T'AI CHI CHIH!

by JUSTIN F. STONE

Printed in the United States of America

Library of Congress Catalog Card Number: 74-80482
ISBN: 0-937277-02-9

Dedicated to
my friend and teacher,
Wen-Shan Huang
(philosopher, anthropologist, T'ai Chi master),
from whom I have learned
so much

Drawings by Ou Mie Shu

CHERRIES

BAMBOO

4

TABLE OF CONTENTS

FOREWORD 8
PART ONE
    INTRODUCTION 12
    PREFACE 18
    INSTRUCTIONAL INTRODUCTION 30
PART TWO
    INSTRUCTION 38
    ROCKING MOTION 40
    BIRD FLAPS ITS WINGS 42
    BASIC LEG MOVEMENTS 46
    AROUND THE PLATTER 50
    AROUND THE PLATTER (VARIATION) 54
    BASS DRUM 58
    DAUGHTER ON THE MOUNTAIN TOP 62
    DAUGHTER IN THE VALLEY 66
    CARRY BALL TO THE SIDE 70
    PUSH PULL 74
    PULLING IN THE ENERGY 78
    PULLING TAFFY (AND VARIATIONS) 82
    WORKING THE PULLEY 96
    LIGHT AT TOP OF THE HEAD 100
    JOYOUS BREATH 104
    PASSING CLOUDS 106
    SIX HEALING SOUNDS 108
    COSMIC CONSCIOUSNESS POSE 118
    OPTIONAL INDIAN DANCE 120
PART THREE
    EPILOGUE 124
    GREAT CIRCLE MEDITATION 130

THE JAPANESE CALL IT 'SEIJAKU', AND THE PEOPLES OF
THE CROWDED ORIENT GENERALLY KNOW THIS FEELING OF
"SERENITY IN THE MIDST OF ACTIVITY". IT IS NOT BY
REFRAINING FROM ACTION THAT WE ACHIEVE IT, BUT BY
MAINTAINING A FIRM, UNCHANGING CENTER IN THE MIDST
OF DISTURBANCE.

WHEN WE DO THE MEASURED MOVEMENTS OF 'T'AI CHI
CHIH,' WHILE FOCUSING OUR CONCENTRATION ON THE SPOT
TWO INCHES BELOW THE NAVEL, WE FEEL THE SURGE OF
VITAL FORCE AND EXPERIENCE A PLEASANT TINGLING —
YET, WHEN WE ARE QUIET AGAIN, THAT CENTER IN THE
SOLAR PLEXUS IS FILLED WITH POWER AND WE FEEL AT
REST. THIS SERENITY SHOULD SPILL OVER INTO OUR
EVERY-DAY LIVES, MAKING POSSIBLE A CALM AND JOYOUS
INTERIOR EVEN DURING THE MOST HECTIC TIMES.

THE CIRCLE REPRESENTS THE 'TAO' OR 'T'AI CHI'
(SUPREME ULTIMATE)

THE WHITE IS THE 'YANG' FORCE
(HEAT, EXPANSION, THE CREATIVE, MALE, POSITIVE)

THE BLACK IS THE 'YIN' FORCE
(COLD, CONTRACTION, THE RECEPTIVE, FEMALE,
NEGATIVE)

FOREWORD

By Steve Ridley, TCC Master

Though I have practised and taught T'ai Chi Chih for several years, I find it very difficult to define. How can one accurately describe that which has been credited with the healing of chronic ailments, the development of dynamic internal energy, the cultivation of inner stability, the awakening of intuitive functioning, wisdom, compassion, and joy?

T'ai Chi Chih is a newly developed system of movement discipline. It consists of 20 individual movement patterns that generate, circulate, and harmonize internal energy flows. This action is said to encourage health restoration and enlightenment. T'ai Chi is often referred to as a "moving meditation," because it reveals inner serenity and tends to refine and expand one's outlook. It is a healing art of the highest caliber, that has strongly contributed to the transformation of many lives. T'ai Chi Chih is all of these things, yet for each practitioner it has special significance.

Justin Stone is the originator of T'ai Chi Chih, or, rather, the inspired channel through which T'ai Chi Chih developed. He is an authority on Oriental systems of meditation and healing. Justin has been a constant source of inspiration to me through the years. He is my close spiritual friend and teacher. Justin is the rarest kind of T'ai Chi teacher, for he *lives* the teaching; he embodies it. He has consistently demonstrated the essence of T'ai Chi by presence and example. Through T'ai Chi Chih, he shares with us the fruition of many years of thorough examination, contemplation, and experimentation. May we have the discernment to recognize the value of what Justin shares and the wisdom to utilize it.

The more that I practise the movements and principles of T'ai Chi Chih, the more profound and mysterious it becomes. I have experienced breakthroughs in understanding and have seen many useful opportunities unfold in my life, as a direct result of my involvements with T'ai Chi Chih. I frequently hear from students and teachers of T'ai Chi Chih who proclaim marked improvements in physical functioning, creativity, mental clarity, emotional stability, vitality and happiness.

I am convinced that if a person will practise T'ai Chi Chih sincerely and correctly on a regular basis, its healing benefits and its life-transforming influence will be known; it cannot be otherwise. The goal of this discipline and its potential promise is stated in its title: T'ai Chi Chih ("knowledge of the Supreme Ultimate"). Justin is usually reluctant to participate in philosophical discussions about T'ai Chi Chih, though he consistently and enthusiastically advises, "Practise, practise, practise!" I sincerely hope that by the study of this text and the application of its contents, you will realize the highest goal.

TREE ON MOUNTAINTOP

10

PART ONE

NEW INTRODUCTION

HAVING PRACTISED THE ANCIENT T'AI CHI CH'UAN FOR MANY YEARS, AND TAUGHT IT AT UNIVERSITIES AND ELSEWHERE, I FINALLY REALIZED THAT THE FORM IS DIFFICULT FOR MOST PEOPLE TO LEARN AND ALMOST IMPOSSIBLE FOR SOME PEOPLE TO DO. THE BENEFITS ARE MANY AND THE SATISFACTIONS GREAT *IF* ONE SPENDS THE LONG TIME NECESSARY TO MASTER IT AND BEGIN TO REALIZE THE EFFECTS OF CIRCULATING AND BALANCING THE CHI, THE INTRINSIC ENERGY SOMETIMES REFERRED TO AS VITAL FORCE. I FOUND, THROUGH CONVERSATIONS WITH OTHER T'AI CHI CH'UAN INSTRUCTORS, THAT FOR EVERY FIFTEEN PEOPLE WHO BEGIN T'AI CHI CH'UAN LESSONS, PERHAPS ONE WILL BE MOTIVATED ENOUGH TO LEARN THE FIRST TWO SECTIONS, AND OFTEN NONE GO ON TO MASTER THE THREE DIVISIONS OF 108 MOVEMENTS IN THE YANG SYSTEM. SO, ALTHOUGH I RECOGNIZED THE BENEFITS OF T'AI CHI CH'UAN PRACTISE AND RECEIVED THESE BENEFITS DAILY, IT WAS ALL TOO APPARENT THAT GREAT NUMBERS OF PEOPLE WOULD NOT DO T'AI CHI CH'UAN, THAT IT WAS FOR A COMPARATIVE FEW IN THIS COUNTRY.

BELIEVING STRONGLY IN THE BENEFITS OF THE ANCIENT YIN-YANG SYSTEM, AND HAVING OBSERVED IN MYSELF THE CONSIDERABLE GAINS FROM CIRCULATION AND BALANCING OF THE CHI, I BEGAN, AROUND 1969, TO EXPERIMENT WITH MY OWN FORMS BASED ON THE ANCIENT PRINCIPLES, FORMS THAT DID NOT HAVE TO BE PERFORMED IN ANY ORDER AND YET WOULD BRING GREAT BENEFITS, EVEN IF ONLY SOME OF THEM WERE LEARNED AND PRACTISED. HAVING BEEN FORTUNATE ENOUGH TO LEARN FROM AN OLD CHINESE SEVERAL LITTLE-KNOWN MOVEMENTS PRACTISED IN FORMER DAYS, I USED THESE AS THE STARTING POINT FOR MY EXPERIMENTS. ONE, LATER KNOWN AS "CIRCLES WITHIN CIRCLES," I DROPPED AS IT SEEMED TOO DIFFICULT FOR THE AVERAGE PERSON TO SUCCESSFULLY PERFORM. THE OTHER TWO MOVEMENTS I CHANGED AND ADDED MY OWN LEG MOVEMENTS, WITH THE "YINNING" AND "YANGING" NOW

SO FAMILIAR TO THE THOUSANDS OF THOSE WHO PRAC-
TISE MY FORM, T'AI CHI CHIH. THESE TWO, ALONG WITH
THE SWINGING MOVEMENT KNOWN AS "ROCKING MOTION,"
I TAUGHT TO MY T'AI CHI CH'UAN STUDENTS TO DO AS
PRELIMINARY, WARM-UP 'EXERCISES' BEFORE BEGINNING
T'AI CHI CH'UAN. THE STUDENTS SEEMED MUCH TAKEN
WITH THE NEW MOVEMENTS, AND THERE WAS CON-
SIDERABLE ENTHUSIASM FOR THEM.

OVER THE NEXT FEW YEARS, A TIME WHEN I PER-
SONALLY WAS DOING CONSIDERABLE MEDITATION AND
OTHER SPIRITUAL PRACTISE, NEW MOVEMENTS CAME TO
ME IN AN EFFORTLESS MANNER. I TRIED TO NAME THEM IN
SIMPLE, DESCRIPTIVE TERMS. WHEN ENOUGH HAD BEEN
PERFECTED, I DECIDED TO CALL THEM, COLLECTIVELY, "T'AI
CHI CHIH," T'AI CHI BEING GENERALLY TRANSLATED AS
"SUPREME ULTIMATE" (SAME AS "TAO") AND THE
CHARACTER FOR CHIH MEANING "KNOWLEDGE" OR
"KNOWING" (CHINESE HAS NO GRAMMAR AND THE SAME
WORD CAN BE A VERB, A NOUN, OR AN ADJECTIVE). SO, WE
WERE NOW DEALING WITH "KNOWLEDGE OF THE SUPREME
ULTIMATE," AND AN APT DESCRIPTION IT IS. MY STUDIES IN
INDIA, JAPAN AND CHINESE CITIES HAD LED ME TO BELIEVE
THAT CONTROL OF THE CHI (KNOWN AS "PRANA" IN INDIA)
WAS THE GREAT SECRET OF LIFE. INDEED, THE INDIAN
SAGE, SRI AURIBINDO, HAD MADE THE AUDACIOUS STATE-
MENT THAT, IF THE UNIVERSE WERE ABOLISHED, THIS CHI
WOULD BE CAPABLE OF CONSTRUCTING A NEW UNIVERSE
IN ITS PLACE! ELSEWHERE IN THIS BOOK, AND IN SOME OF
MY OTHER BOOKS, I COMMENT IN GREATER DETAIL ABOUT
THIS CHI AND WHAT IT REALLY IS AND DOES.

IN 1974, SUN PUBLISHING CO. ASKED ME TO WRITE
A BOOK ON T'AI CHI CH'UAN, MY FIRST TWO BOOKS ("THE
JOYS OF MEDITATION" AND "ABAONDON HOPE!") HAVING
BEEN UNEXPECTEDLY SUCCESSFUL FOR THEM. I DECLINED
AND COUNTERED WITH THE SUGGESTION THAT I DO A
BOOK, THE FIRST BOOK, ON "T'AI CHI CHIH." THIS SUGGES-
TION WAS ENTHUSIASTICALLY ACCEPTED, AND I BEGAN THE
LABORIOUS TASK OF FINISHING AND NAMING THE NINE-
TEEN FORMS WHICH APPEARED IN THE FIRST T'AI CHI CHIH
BOOK (LATER, "BIRD FLAPS ITS WINGS" WAS ADDED, MAK-
ING TWENTY IN ALL). WHEN THIS TASK WAS COMPLETED, I

BEGAN TO WRITE THE BOOK, WHICH FEATURED A FOREWARD BY THE GREAT CHINESE SCHOLAR, WEN SHAN HUANG, AND WORKED WITH SUN PUBLISHING CO. TO PRODUCE THE NECESSARY PHOTOGRAPHS. THE TASK WAS COMPLETED, AND THE BOOK PUBLISHED, A FEW MONTHS BEFORE THE FIRST FORMAL LESSONS IN T'AI CHI CHIH WERE GIVEN IN ALBUQUERQUE, NEW MEXICO.

NATURALLY, T'AI CHI CHIH TEACHING METHODS HAVE EVOLVED AS CLASSES PROLIFERATED, AND THE ORDER IN WHICH THE MOVEMENTS WERE TAUGHT GRADUALLY CHANGED UNTIL THEY HAVE STABILIZED IN THE SEQUENCE GIVEN IN THIS NEW, REVISED EDITION.

IN AUGUST, 1975, T'AI CHI CHIH TEACHERS' TRAINING CLASSES BEGAN AND HAVE CONTINUED EVER SINCE AT AN AVERAGE OF THREE OR FOUR A YEAR. HERE EAGER ASPIRANTS WHO HAD MASTERED T'AI CHI CHIH FORMS, AND WHO WERE RECEIVING THE BENEFITS FROM THEIR OWN PRACTISE, ATTENDED CONCENTRATED COURSES DESIGNED TO SHOW THEM HOW TO TEACH TCC AND CONSTRUCTED SO AS TO GIVE THEM BACKGROUND KNOWLEDGE OF THE PHILOSOPHY ON WHICH T'AI CHI CHIH IS BASED. AS OF THE END OF 1981, ABOUT 160 INSTRUCTORS HAVE BEEN ACCREDITED BY ME AFTER SUCCESSFULLY COMPLETING THE NECESSARY TRAINING. THEY IN TURN WENT TO WORK WITH THEIR OWN STUDENTS IN THEIR OWN CLASSES AS THEY FANNED OUT ACROSS THE UNITED STATES AND THROUGH SOME FOREIGN COUNTRIES, SUCH AS SWITZERLAND, WEST GERMANY, CHILE AND CANADA. MUCH HAS BEEN LEARNED FROM *THEIR* EXPERIENCES IN TEACHING, AND I AM GRATEFUL TO THEM FOR ADVANCING OUR KNOWLEDGE OF THIS NEW FORM, NOW ONLY EIGHT YEARS OLD.

WHEN IT BECAME APPARENT THAT THE ORDER IN WHICH TCC MOVEMENTS ARE TAUGHT IN CLASS WAS SOMEWHAT DIFFERENT FROM THE WAY THEY APPEARED IN THE ORIGINAL YELLOW-COVERED BOOK, IT WAS OBVIOUS THAT A REVISED EDITION WOULD HAVE TO BE COMPILED, TO BRING IN THE NEW MOVEMENTS ("BIRD FLAPS ITS WINGS" AND THE "SIX HEALING SOUNDS" MOVEMENTS), AND TO ADJUST THE ORDER OF MOVEMENTS IN THE BOOK TO THAT WHICH NOW PREDOMINATES IN CLASS TEACHING.

THESE NEW DEVELOPMENTS HAD EVOLVED FROM ACTUAL TEACHING EXPERIENCES, AND IT IS NECESSARY THAT TCC, LIKE ALL GROWING FORMS, EVOLVE AND NOT REMAIN STAGNANT. TO REMAIN UNCHANGING IS TO DIE.

THIS BOOK HAS BEEN WRITTEN TO FILL THAT NEED. AS MENTIONED, THE MOVEMENTS PERFORMED WITH THE SIX HEALING SOUNDS HAVE CHANGED SLIGHTLY, AND "BIRD FLAPS ITS WINGS" WAS ADDED TO THE ORIGINAL NINETEEN MOVEMENTS. THE OVERLY DIFFICULT "CIRCLES WITHIN CIRCLES," WHICH IS NOT TAUGHT IN CLASSES, HAS BEEN REMOVED FROM THIS REVISED EDITION. T'AI CHI CHIH IS JUSTIFIABLY CALLED "JOY THROUGH MOVEMENT," AND WE WANT IT TO BE FUN; THERE IS NO NEED TO FORCE DIF-FICULT FORMS ON THE BEGINNING STUDENT. ACTUALLY, THE PRACTISE OF ANY TEN OF THE TWENTY MOVEMENTS AND POSTURES, IF REPEATED REGULARLY, SHOULD BE ENOUGH TO BRING GREAT RESULTS, BUT, OF COURSE, IT IS MORE ADVANTAGEOUS TO LEARN *ALL* THE MOVEMENTS AND GET THE BENEFITS FROM EACH. IT IS FELT THAT THIS BOOK NOW FAITHFULLY COINCIDES WITH THE TCC THAT IS TAUGHT BY THE TEACHERS IN CLASSES, AND, WHETHER THE READER LEARNS BY HIMSELF, FROM THIS BOOK, OR STUDIES IN THE TCC CLASSES, HE SHOULD FIND THE BOOK TO BE A FAITHFUL TEXT.

THIS IS THE BACKGROUND ON HOW T'AI CHI CHIH CAME INTO BEING AND WHY THIS NEW BOOK WAS WRIT-TEN. THESE ARE NOT ANCIENT FORMS; THEY WERE ORIGINATED BY ME, BUT THEY DO USE THE VERY OLD YIN-YANG PRINCIPLES AND A FEW IDEAS FROM T'AI CHI CH'UAN. THE PURPOSE WAS, AND IS, TO PROVIDE EASILY LEARNED MOVEMENTS THAT AFFORD THE PRACTISER GREAT BENEFITS. HOW GREAT THESE BENEFITS ARE— SPIRITUALLY, PHYSICALLY AND PSYCHOLOGICALLY— WE DID NOT KNOW AT THE BEGINNING, AND IT HAS BEEN GRATIFYING THROUGH THE YEARS TO CONSTANTLY RECEIVE NEW REPORTS OF HITHERTO UNSUSPECTED BENEFITS EXPERIENCED BY THOSE LEARNING TCC.

WHETHER ONE UNDERSTANDS THE REASONS FOR SUCH BENEFITS OR NOT, AND WHETHER OR NOT ONE HAS FAITH, REGULAR PRACTICE OF TCC SHOULD BRING GREAT REWARDS. JUST DO IT AND LET YOUR OWN EXPERIENCE

CONVINCE YOU. MANY HAVE STATED THAT THEY LIKE TCC BECAUSE NO BELIEFS ARE NEEDED AND WORDS PLAY NO PART IN SUCCESSFUL PRACTISE. TRULY, THE AIM IS "JOY THROUGH MOVEMENT," AND SUCH MOVEMENT IS EASY. MOREOVER, THE COMPLETE FORM CAN EASILY BE LEARNED IN THE EIGHT OR TEN LESSONS USUALLY CONSTITUTING A COMPLETE BEGINNER'S COURSE, WHICH TAKES MERELY A MATTER OF A FEW WEEKS TO COMPLETE. T'AI CHI CHIH CAN BE A LOVING, AS WELL AS A HEALING, EXPERIENCE. TEACHERS' TRAINING ASPIRANTS DO NOT SOON FORGET THE GREAT FEELING OF WARMTH THAT GROWS BETWEEN THEMSELVES AND THEIR INSTRUCTORS, AND MOST SEEM TO LEAVE THE TEACHERS' COURSES ON A REAL HIGH, WHICH, HOPEFULLY, THEY PASS ALONG TO THEIR STUDENTS. WE TRUST THE READER OF THIS BOOK WILL JOIN US IN THIS SIMPLE PRACTISE. IF ENOUGH PEOPLE DO T'AI CHI CHIH, WE MIGHT EVEN HAVE PEACE AND LOVE IN THE WORLD.

CATTAILS

PREFACE

WHAT ARE THE GREAT SECRETS OF LIFE? PERHAPS THERE ARE FEW OF THEM. PROBABLY NONE IS MORE IMPORTANT THAN THE KNOWLEDGE OF HOW TO CIRCULATE AND BALANCE THE INTRINSIC ENERGY, THE VITAL FORCE OF THE BODY, KNOWN AS 'CHI' IN CHINESE. THE REWARDS IN GOOD HEALTH, WISDOM, SERENITY, AND LONGEVITY ARE GREAT FOR THE ONE WHO LEARNS THE ANCIENT PRINCIPLES AND APPLIES THEM IN A MODERN WAY. SO LITTLE OF SUCH ARTS IS KNOWN IN THE WEST, BUT NOW, STIMULATED BY THE GROWTH OF MEDITATION PRACTICE AND THE INTENSE INTEREST IN ACUPUNCTURE, PEOPLE HAVE BEGUN TO TURN TO ANCIENT CHINESE 'T'AI CHI CH'UAN', HATHA YOGA, ETC., ETC. FOR SELF-CULTURE.

AS A 'T'AI CHI CH'UAN' INSTRUCTOR, I AM VERY ENTHUSIASTIC ABOUT TEACHING THIS DISCIPLINE, AND ALWAYS SEEM TO HAVE A WAITING LIST FOR NEW CLASSES. AND YET, I REALIZE THAT IT TAKES MANY MONTHS OF HARD WORK TO LEARN THE 108 MOVEMENTS OF 'T'AI CHI CH'UAN'. ONCE LEARNED, IT TAKES AT LEAST 12 FEET OF SPACE IN WHICH TO PRACTISE. OLDER PEOPLE HAVE SOME DIFFICULTY EXECUTING THE MOVEMENTS, AS WELL AS A PROBLEM IN MEMORIZING THE LONG SEQUENCE. AND, FINALLY, 'T'AI CHI CH'UAN', WONDERFUL AS IT IS, CANNOT BE LEARNED FROM A BOOK — A PERSONAL INSTRUCTOR IS ABSOLUTELY NECESSARY.

IN CONTRAST, 'T'AI CHI CHIH' CAN EASILY BE
LEARNED FROM THIS BOOK. ANY SIX OF THE MOVEMENTS,
PRACTISED 36 TIMES ON THE LEFT SIDE AND 36 TIMES ON
THE RIGHT SIDE, SHOULD AFFORD GREAT BENEFITS. VERY
LITTLE SPACE IS NEEDED; ONE CAN STAND AT HIS DESK
WHENEVER HE FEELS DROWSY AND, REACHING OUT ONLY
TO ARMS LENGTH, RE-STIMULATE HIMSELF BY LEISURELY
DOING A FEW OF THE MOVEMENTS. THEY ARE SO GENTLE,
AND TAKE SO LITTLE CO-ORDINATION, THAT PEOPLE OF
ANY AGE CAN EASILY DO THEM. ALL THAT IS NEEDED IS
TO PRACTISE THE MOVEMENTS REGULARLY, 10 OR 15
MINUTES IN THE MORNING AND 10 OR 15 MINUTES IN THE
LATE AFTERNOON OR EARLY EVENING. PROPERLY DONE,
THE RESULT SHOULD BE A FLOW OF ENERGY AND A
FEELING OF WELL-BEING SOMEWHAT LIKE THE AFTERMATH
OF AN INTERNAL BATH. THE FIRST MANIFESTATION IS
USUALLY A TINGLING IN THE FINGERS AND A FEELING OF
FULLNESS AND ENERGY-FLOW IN THE HANDS. IF THE
MENTAL CONCENTRATION IS KEPT IN THE SOLES OF THE
FEET (THE SO-CALLED 'BUBBLING SPRING') OR TWO INCHES
BELOW THE NAVEL (THE 'TAN T'IEN', PRONOUNCED
'DANTIEN'), THE FLOW WILL EVENTUALLY SURGE THRU
THE BODY, AND A FEELING OF HEAT MAY SUDDENLY
APPEAR IN THE ARMS, AT THE BASE OF THE SKULL, OR
ELSEWHERE. A VIBRATION MAY BEGIN IN THE SOLES OF
THE FEET, OR AT THE SOLAR PLEXUS, AND THERE MAY BE
A FEELING THAT THE HAIRS AT THE TOP OF THE NECK
ARE STANDING UP. A STRONG TWITCHING IS OFTEN FELT
IN THE FOREHEAD JUST ABOVE AND BETWEEN THE EYES,
A SPOT USUALLY REFERRED TO IN OCCULT CIRCLES AS
'THE THIRD EYE'. EACH PERSON WILL FEEL THE SURGE OF
VITAL FORCE IN HIS OWN WAY, AND IT IS A PLEASANT
FEELING. THIS HEAT CURRENT IS ALSO SAID TO BE VERY
HEALING IN NATURE, AND THE WRITER CAN ATTEST TO
SUCH RESULT IN HIS OWN PARTICULAR CASE AS REGARDS
A CHRONIC AILMENT, PROBABLY RESULTING FROM INJURY.

ABOVE ALL, WE TEND TO 'WAKE UP', TO FEEL GOOD AND MORE ALIVE. IN THIS RESPECT, 'T'AI CHI CHIH' IS LIKE A VALUABLE MEDITATION.

WHAT IS THIS VITAL FORCE THAT WE BECOME AWARE OF, THE FLOW OF INTRINSIC ENERGY SEEMING TO ARISE WITHIN US? THE CHINESE, THOSE PEOPLE OF GREAT VITALITY, CALL IT 'CHI'. IT IS KNOWN AS 'KI' IN JAPAN, WHERE IT IS THE BASIS FOR HIGHER 'AIKIDO' AND OTHER MARTIAL ARTS. THE WISE MEN OF INDIA HAVE REFERRED TO IT VARIOUSLY AS 'SAKTI', 'KUNDALINI', AND 'PRANA'. IN INDIAN TANTRIC PRACTICES, THIS ENERGY AS 'SAKTI' (THE ACTIVE FORCE OF THE REALITY, 'SHIVA') IS ACTUALLY WORSHIPED. TAKING THIS ENERGY UP ALONG THE SPINE, OPENING THE PSYCHIC CENTERS, IS THE WAY FOR MEN TO BECOME GODS, IN THE KUNDALINI PRACTICE OF HINDU TANTRA, BUT THIS MUST BE DONE UNDER CLOSE SUPERVISION OF A PERFECT MASTER (GURU), SO ITS POSSIBILITIES ARE LIMITED TO ONLY A FEW.

IT IS INTERESTING THAT THE CHINESE USE THE WORD 'CHI' AS TRANSLATION FOR THE INDIAN SANSKRIT 'PRANA', ALL THE FORCE OF THE UNIVERSE, THE POWER THAT BREATHES US AND MAKES US LIVE (THIS SAME FORCE IS EXPRESSED, UNFORTUNATELY, IN THE ATOM BOMB). THIS 'CHI' IS ALSO USED AS TRANSLATION FOR THE SANSKRIT WORD 'PRAJNA', WHICH MEANS WISDOM IN THE GREATER SENSE. SO THE VITAL FORCE, THIS INTRINSIC ENERGY, IS ALSO THE WISDOM THAT IS THE DEEP-ROOTED SOURCE OF INTUITION. A LONG-TIME PRACTISER OF 'T'AI CHI CHIH' WILL KNOW WELL WHAT THE ANCIENTS MEANT WHEN THEY SAID: "TO UNITE THE DIVINE ENERGY WITHIN ME WITH THE UNIVERSAL ENERGY, THAT IS THE GOAL!"

HAKUIN ZENJI, THE 18TH CENTURY JAPANESE ZEN MASTER (AND PERHAPS THE MOST INFLUENTIAL IN JAPAN'S LONG HISTORY OF BUDDHISM), TELLS A CURIOUS STORY IN HIS LITTLE-KNOWN WORK, "YASENKANNA". TIRED AND IN EXTREMELY BAD HEALTH FROM HIS ARDUOUS MEDITATIONS

AND LONG SEARCH FOR TRUTH, HAKUIN HEARD ABOUT
A SENNIN, A MOUNTAIN MASTER, LIVING IN SECLUSION
NEAR SHIROKAWA (WHITE RIVER JUNCTION) IN THE
MOUNTAINS OF JAPAN. HE PROMPTLY MADE A PILGRIM-
AGE THERE AND, AFTER DIFFICULTY IN FINDING THE
MASTER (WHO WAS LIVING IN A CAVE IN THE REMOTE
RECESSES OF THE MOUNTAINS), HE FINALLY CAME
FACE-TO-FACE WITH HIM IN HIS SMALL RETREAT.
HAKUIN WAS SURPRISED TO SEE NO FOOD AT ALL IN
THE CAVE, AND HE KNEW, FROM THE VILLAGERS,
THAT HAKUYU, THE MASTER, HAD NOT LEFT THERE
FOR SOME TIME. MOREOVER, THE OLDER MAN (SOME
SAID HE HAD BEEN THE TEACHER OF ANOTHER GREAT
MASTER OVER A HUNDRED YEARS BEFORE!) WAS
WEARING BUT A THIN COVERING, CURLED WITH COLD
(THE AUTHOR CAN ATTEST TO THE FREEZING WINTER
WEATHER IN THOSE MOUNTAINS!), AND YET DID NOT
SEEM TO NOTICE THE CHILL AT ALL. HE WAS KNEELING
IN MEDITATION WHEN HAKUIN ENTERED THE CAVE,
PRACTISING THE SECRET NAIKAN DISCIPLINE (EXPLAINED
AS 'NEI KUNG', THE CHINESE PRONUNCIATION, IN MY
BOOK "THE JOYS OF MEDITATION") THAT IS PART OF
THE 'CHI KUNG' SERIES OF PRACTICES, JUST AS 'T'AI
CHI CHIH' IS. THESE ARE DESIGNED TO ACTIVATE,
CIRCULATE, AND BALANCE THE DIVINE ENERGY (CHI)
LYING DORMANT IN EACH ONE OF US.

HAKUYU TAUGHT THIS CIRCULATION OF THE CHI
TO HAKUIN, BOTH TO HELP HIS RAPIDLY-DEGENERATING
HEALTH AND TO ENABLE HIM TO MAKE A BREAKTHRU
IN HIS CONTEMPLATIONS, NECESSARY FOR HIM TO
REACH FULL ENLIGHTENMENT. HAKUIN WRITES THAT,
USING THIS METHOD OF CIRCULATING AND BALANCING
THE 'CHI', HE SUCCEEDED IN BOTH ENDEAVORS AND
WENT ON TO BECOME ONE OF THE GREATEST ZEN
MASTERS THE ORIENT HAS KNOWN. SINCE HAKUIN
WAS ONE OF THE MOST NOTABLE RELIGIOUS FIGURES

IN JAPANESE HISTORY, AND SINCE HE WAS OF A PEOPLE WELL-KNOWN FOR THEIR UNDERSTATEMENT, CAN WE DOUBT HIS WORD WHEN HE ATTESTS TO THE EFFICACY OF THE FLOWING 'CHI'?

WHEN WE SPEAK OF "BALANCING" THIS INTRINSIC ENERGY (WHICH CHINESE ZENNISTS SOMETIMES OBSCURELY REFERRED TO AS "YOUR ORIGINAL FACE"), WE MEAN BRINGING THE YIN AND YANG ELEMENTS INTO BALANCE. IN CHINESE COSMOLOGY, WE HAVE THE INEFFABLE 'TAO' (ALSO KNOWN AS 'T'AI CHI'), THE SUPREME ULTIMATE ABOUT WHICH NOTHING CAN BE PREDICATED. FROM THIS MATRIX COME THE YIN AND THE YANG, WHICH CAN BE CALLED THE NEGATIVE AND THE POSITIVE, THE RECEPTIVE AND THE CREATIVE, THE COLD AND THE HOT, THE INSUBSTANTIAL AND THE SUB-STANTIAL, ETC. — THE FORCES OF THE TWO POLARITIES. THEN, FROM THE YIN AND YANG WE GET HEAVEN ABOVE, EARTH BELOW, AND MAN IN THE CENTER (THIS IS WHY JAPANESE FLOWER ARRANGEMENTS ARE GENERALLY THREE-POINTED). FROM THESE DERIVE THE 10,000 THINGS, THE WORLD OF DIVERSIFIED PHENOMENA PERCEIVED BY THE SENSES.

THE ANCIENT TEACHING IS THAT THE 'YIN' (FEMALE) AND 'YANG' (MALE) ELEMENTS SEPARATE WHEN IN MOTION, AND COME TOGETHER AGAIN IN QUIESCENCE. SO, WHEN WE BEGIN THE MOTIONS OF 'T'AI CHI CHIH', WE ARE DIVIDING THE TWO FORCES; THEN WE BALANCE THEM AS WE PRACTISE. FINALLY, WHEN WE ARE STILL AGAIN, THEY REUNITE.

OFTEN WE SEE THE GREAT TEACHING REPRESENTED BY THE BALL THAT APPEARS LIKE THIS:

THIS IS THE 'TAO', OR 'T'AI CHI'. NOTICE THAT IN THE BLACK (THE FEMALE OR NEGATIVE) THERE IS A FAINT SPOT OF WHITE, AND, CONVERSELY, IN THE WHITE (THE MALE OR POSITIVE), THERE IS A FAINT SPOT OF BLACK. THUS THERE IS ALWAYS SOME FEMALE IN THE MALE, AND VICE VERSA. IT IS THIS WHICH MAKES POSSIBLE THE BALANCING OF THE 'CHI'.

THE CHINESE SAY THAT WHEN ONE FORCE IS CARRIED TO EXTREMES (GROWS TOO STRONG), IT TURNS INTO ITS OPPOSITE. THIS IS POSSIBLE BECAUSE YIN AND YANG ATTRACT EACH OTHER. SO, TOO MUCH 'YANG' (POSITIVE) EVENTUALLY BECOMES 'YIN' (NEGATIVE). WE CAN EASILY IDENTIFY THIS IN OUR OWN WORLD, WHERE IT IS SAID, "PLEASURE INDEFINITELY PROLONGED BECOMES PAIN." ONE ICE CREAM SODA TASTES GOOD, BUT TEN ICE CREAM SODAS MAKE US SICK. AND SO IT IS SAID THAT "THE WISE MAN GOES TO HIS TRIUMPH LIKE A FUNERAL", KNOWING THE GREATEST HIGH EVENTUALLY TURNS INTO A LOW. THE SAGE HAS SAID, IF YOU WANT TO LIFT ANYTHING, FIRST PUSH DOWN ON IT TO BREAK THE ATTACHMENT. THE 'YANG' (CREATIVE) IS THE FATHER OF ALL THINGS, BUT THE 'YIN' (RECEPTIVE), IS THE GREAT MOTHER. EACH EVENTUALLY TURNS INTO ITS OPPOSITE, AND BOTH ARE ALWAYS PRESENT TO SOME DEGREE.

WATER, AND MOST FLUID, IS STRONGLY 'YIN', AND, WHEN WE HAVE AN EXCESS OF FLUID IN OUR SYSTEMS, WE ARE TOO 'YIN' AND TEND TOWARD ILLNESS. THE FLOW OF THE 'CHI' IN 'T'AI CHI CHIH' HELPS DRY THIS EXCESS FLUID, SO WE TEND TO LOSE WEIGHT IF WE ARE FAT AND TO HAVE BETTER HEALTH AS THIS EXTRA 'YIN' IS REMOVED. WE ARE USUALLY THIRSTY AFTER PRACTISING 'T'AI CHI CHIH' BECAUSE OF THIS DRYING EFFECT. IT IS BEST NOT TO DRINK SOMETHING COLD IMMEDIATELY AFTER FINISHING, AS WE HAVE BEEN

EXERCISING THE INTERNAL ORGANS AND PRODUCING A SUBTLE HEAT IN THEM.

WHEN WE FIRST START THE MOVEMENTS OF 'T'AI CHI CHIH', WE ARE BEGINNING TO CIRCULATE THE 'CHI'. AS WE EMPHASIZE RIGHT OR LEFT IN THE HANDS, TO BALANCE THE SUBSTANTIAL OR INSUBSTANTIAL POSITION OF THE LEGS (THRU THE KNEES), WE ARE BALANCING THIS VITAL FORCE AS IT FLOWS. THEN, WHEN WE COME TO REST, THE 'YIN' AND 'YANG' ELEMENTS RE-UNITE AND ARE STORED IN THE BONES, ACCORDING TO THE OLD CHINESE TEACHING. IT IS THIS STORED 'CHI' ENERGY THAT ENABLES A MASTER OF KARATE, AIKIDO, OR ONE OF THE OTHER MARTIAL ART DISCIPLINES, TO SMASH HIS HAND THRU A CON-CRETE BLOCK, A STUNT WITNESSED MANY TIMES BY WESTERNERS (NOT TOO LONG AGO A BUILDING WAS WRECKED IN JAPAN IN THIS MANNER, USING ONLY THE HANDS OF A FEW ADEPTS WHO VOLUNTEERED THEIR SERVICES). IT IS NOT MUSCULAR FORCE HE USES; YOU WILL NOTE HE USUALLY LETS OUT A SHARP CRY AS HE MUSTERS THE STORED 'CHI' AND THEN SMASHES HIS HAND THRU THE OBSTACLE. CONCENTRATING ON THE T'AN T'IEN (TWO INCHES BELOW THE NAVEL) WILL CAUSE A GOOD DEAL OF 'CHI' TO BE STORED THERE, THE SEAT OF HEAVEN. THERE ARE AIKIDO CLUBS IN JAPAN THAT GO SWIMMING ON THE COLDEST WINTER DAYS, KEEPING INTENSE CONCENTRATION ON THE HEAT-MAKING 'CHI' STORED IN THE SPOT BELOW THE NAVEL ("TANDEN" IN JAPANESE).

SHALL I RELATE ONE MORE STORY TO SHOW THE WONDROUS PROPERTIES OF THE 'CHI'? IT IS A STORY THAT WAS TOLD TO ME (I WAS NOT THERE), BUT ONE THAT IS FAIRLY COMMON IN CIRCLES OF THIS ORIENTAL DISCIPLINE.

TWO BLACK BELT JUDO ADEPTS HEARD THAT AN OLDER MASTER WAS COMING TO A CITY CLOSE TO

THEIRS. THEY MADE A HURRIED TRIP THERE TO PAY
THEIR RESPECTS, AND WERE SOMEWHAT DISAPPOINTED
TO FIND A TINY, OLDER MAN, PERHAPS WEIGHING LESS
THAN 100 POUNDS. THE FIRST JUDO MAN, OVER SIX
FEET TALL AND QUITE MUSCULAR, SAID TO THE
MASTER: "ALL MY LIFE I HAVE BEEN HEARING ABOUT
THE POWER OF THIS 'CHI'. WOULD YOU BE KIND ENOUGH
TO DEMONSTRATE THE POWER TO US?"

THE MASTER THOUGHT FOR A MOMENT. "I'LL TELL
YOU WHAT," HE BEGAN, "YOU TWO COME AT ME FROM
DIFFERENT DIRECTIONS AND THROW ME DOWN!"

THE TWO BIG MEN, MUCH YOUNGER THAN THE
LITTLE FELLOW, WERE ASTONISHED. "WE'LL KILL YOU!"
EXCLAIMED ONE OF THEM.

"AND DO ME THE HONOR OF NOT TAKING IT EASY
WITH ME!" CONTINUED THE MASTER.

THE TWO JUDO MEN HUDDLED TO DISCUSS THE
TURN OF EVENTS. "YOU FLIP HIM AND I'LL CATCH HIM
BEFORE HE HITS THE MAT", SUGGESTED ONE, AND THE
OTHER NODDED. "WE DON'T WANT TO HURT THE LITTLE
FELLOW."

THE TWO SEPARATED, TURNED, AND BEGAN TO
ADVANCE ON THE MASTER, WATCHING HIS BREATHING
AND WAITING FOR THE RIGHT TIME TO SPRING. WHEN
THEY DID MOVE, IT WAS QUICKLY — AND THEN, I AM
TOLD, THE SPECTATORS SAW A STRANGE SIGHT. ONE
MAN WAS IMMEDIATELY SEEN LYING ON THE GROUND
TEN FEET AWAY, HIS GLASSES KNOCKED OFF, "LOOKING
FOR THE FREIGHT TRAIN" AS HE PUT IT. THE OTHER
HAD STAGGERED BACK AGAINST THE WALL, AND A
SMALL FLECK OF BLOOD APPEARED AT HIS NOSTRILS.
WHAT IS MOST SURPRISING IS THAT NONE OF THE
ASSEMBLED SPECTATORS HAD SEEN THE LITTLE MAN
MOVE AT ALL!

THIS, OF COURSE, IS AN EXTREME EXAMPLE OF
THE EFFECTIVE USE OF THE VITAL FORCE. AND YET,

IT IS LATENT IN ALL OF US. THE STORING OF THIS
FORCE BELOW THE NAVEL IS WHAT ENABLES THE
HOLY MAN, IN TIBET OR NORTHERN INDIA, TO WALK
THRU THE SNOW AND ICE ON THE COLDEST DAYS,
COMFORTABLY WEARING NOTHING BUT A LOIN
CLOTH. IT IS KNOWN AS THE "DUMO HEAT" IN
TIBETAN TANTRIC BUDDHISM. AND IT IS THE FORCE
USED BY HEALERS, WHO MAY IMPART IT AS A
HEALING ENERGY (FELT AS HEAT) BY A TECHNIQUE
OF LAYING-ON-OF-HANDS, OR SOMETHING SIMILAR
(AS IN THE VERY EFFECTIVE JOHREI OF THE
JAPANESE HEALING CHURCH, SEKAI KYUSEI KYO).
THIS SAME ENERGY THAT SEEMS TO HEAL IS THE
BASIS OF ALL SEXUAL VIGOR, WHICH IS SAID TO
BE GREATLY ENHANCED BY THE PRACTISE OF
'T'AI CHI CHIH'.

SO, CIRCULATION AND BALANCE OF THE 'CHI'
ENERGY IS ONE OF THE GREAT SECRETS OF LIFE,
OPEN TO ANY OF US WHO WILL MAKE THE EFFORT.
MOST DO NOT HAVE THE TIME (OR INCLINATION)
TO PRACTISE EXTREME DISCIPLINES, SUCH AS
TANTRIC KUNDALINI YOGA OR ADVANCED HATHA
YOGA. NEVERTHELESS, WE CAN BALANCE AND
CIRCULATE THIS INTRINSIC LIFE FORCE (WHICH
THE GREAT INDIAN PHILOSOPHER, SHANKARA,
CALLED "THE 'REAL' ") THRU THE SIMPLE
PRACTICE OF 'T'AI CHI CHIH'. IF THE STUDENT
PRACTISES FAITHFULLY, THE RESULTS CAN BE
GREAT. WITHOUT MAKING MUCH EFFORT, WE
CANNOT HOPE TO ACHIEVE MUCH. REPETITION
IS IMPORTANT. REGULAR PRACTICE IS NEEDED
TO YIELD RESULTS — AND IT IS WELL WORTH THE
EFFORT! SO, IN THIS WAY, WE CAN UTILIZE ONE
OF THE GREAT SECRETS OF LIFE.

BIRDS FLYING

27

IMPORTANT NOTES ON THE CORRECT PRACTISE OF T'AI CHI CHIH

It is of utmost importance that T'ai Chi Chih be practised correctly in accordance with the principles of YIN-YANG, so that results will be maximized. This means that posture should be correct and that movements be made in the manner that is best described as "Slow Motion in a Dream," or as "Swimming Through Very Heavy Air." One stands with the tailbone pressed slightly forward, and the T'an T'ien (two inches below the navel) compressed against the backbone. The shoulders are relaxed and drooping, and the hands and wrists (more than the arms) move in soft, circular motions. "Softness and Continuity" are necessary. Any tension will keep the Chi (Intrinsic Energy) from flowing freely through the Meridian Channels. The slow-motion, soft, effortless movements will bring desired results, and the leg motions are more important than those of the wrists and hands. Breathing is natural. And it must be remembered that T'ai Chi Chih is not a dance! Long, sweeping, "graceful" movements are apt to be all Yin, or all Yang, thus negating the practice.

Justin Stone originated T'ai Chi Chih, and, at this time, all known teachers are those accredited by him. First they studied—and subsequently practised—the twenty movements, then took intensive Teachers' Training Classes with Justin Stone. Not all those who took such classes were accredited, however. If the reader is to study with a teacher (in a group or singly), it is best that he be sure the teacher is a Justin Stone-accredited teacher. Self-proclaimed teachers do not have the experience nor the understanding of the complex principles involved, and nobody has approved their own personal practise in the traditional Oriental manner. Justin Stone went through many years of study in the Orient—in India, Japan, Chinese cities, etc.—to arrive at the intuitive understanding necessary to originate T'ai Chi Chih.

One other point: it is necessary that the practiser keep his concentration in the soles of his feet (easy) or on the spot two inches below the navel (difficult) while doing the movements. The "Heart Fire" (the Great Yang of the Heart, corresponding to the Yang of the Sun) should be brought down, otherwise the Yin of the Kidneys (corresponding to the Yin of the Moon) will rise. It is not desirable to have the water section floating upward. The great benefits as to health, increased energy and serenity, come from bringing the Heart Fire down as the CHI circulates. When the reader becomes familiar with the practise, these points will become clear to him. Many have learned T'ai Chi Chih from the book alone, but it is helpful to have instruction by fully accredited teachers.

INSTRUCTIONAL INTRODUCTION

THE MOVEMENTS, AND THEIR VARIATIONS, THAT YOU ARE ABOUT TO LEARN ARE THE RESULTS OF MANY YEARS OF EXPERIMENTATION. FROM A DEVELOPMENT OF THE ORIGINAL TWO MOVEMENTS SHOWN ME, ADDING THE LEG MOTIONS AND MAKING OTHER CHANGES, I EXPANDED AND ADDED EIGHTEEN MORE, GIVING THEM DESCRIPTIVE NAMES WHEREVER POSSIBLE. DRAWING ON MY MEDITATION EX-PERIENCES AND T'AI CHI CH'UAN TRAINING, I INTUITIVELY DEVISED THE OTHER MOVEMENTS, SOME OF WHICH VAGUE-LY RESEMBLE PARTS OF T'AI CHI CH'UAN. THIS IS NOT SUR-PRISING, AS BOTH ARE CHI KUNG DISCIPLINES, BASED ON THE GREAT YIN-YANG PRINCIPLES.

SINCE THE FIRST LESSONS IN TCC WERE GIVEN IN 1974, THERE HAVE BEEN MANY REPORTS OF WONDROUS HEAL-INGS AND GRATIFYING SPIRITUAL EXPERIENCES. AN EXCEP-TIONAL LADY IN NORTHERN CALIFORNIA SUFFERED FROM BONE CANCER OF THE LEG, AND HAD TO TAKE HER FIRST LESSONS IN TCC WHILE SEATED. BY THE END OF HER EIGHT-LESSON COURSE, TAKEN WITH A VERY GOOD TEACHER, SHE WAS STANDING AND DOING THE LEG MOVEMENTS. SUBSEQUENT INTENSIVE PRACTISE BROUGHT GREAT IMPROVEMENT IN HER CONDITION AND SHE HAD THE COURAGE TO GO ON AND TAKE THE INTENSIVE TEACHERS' TRAINING COURSE. TODAY SHE IS AN EFFEC-TIVE, ACCREDITED TEACHER, WITH MANY CHANGES IN HER LIFE. SHE IS NOT THE ONLY ONE TO HAVE HAD SUCH AN EX-PERIENCE, THOUGH THE REAL BENEFITS OF T'AI CHI CHIH GO FAR BEYOND SUCH PHYSICAL WELFARE. PEOPLE WITH HIGH BLOOD PRESSURE, WEIGHT PROBLEMS, SEXUAL DIF-FICULTIES, AND MANY OTHER CHRONIC AILMENTS REPORT

QUICK AND MARKED IMPROVEMENT. THE SECRET IS TO DO THE MOVEMENTS CORRECTLY AND TO PRACTISE REGULARLY.

IT IS IMPORTANT TO MAINTAIN COMPLETE RELAXATION WHILE DOING THE MOVEMENTS, AS MUSCULAR TENSION WOULD PREVENT THE 'CHI' FROM FLOWING THROUGH THE PROPER CHANNELS. AGAIN AND AGAIN MY STUDENTS HEAR ME ADVISE "SOFTNESS AND CONTINUITY." EVENTUALLY IT SINKS IN AND THEY GET THE IDEA THAT I MEAN "SOFTNESS AND CONTINUITY." NICE AND EVEN, LIKE THE CHEWING OF FOOD, IS ONE DESCRIPTION THE ANCIENT TEACHERS USED.

THOUGH WE ARE RELAXED AND THE HANDS ARE SOFT, THE AIR IS FELT TO BE VERY HEAVY AS THE HANDS MOVE THROUGH IT, FINGERS SPREAD APART. THIS MAY APPEAR CONTRADICTORY, BUT IT IS NOT. IT IS EASY TO FEEL THE AIR AS HEAVY AND STILL KEEP THE HANDS SLIGHTLY CUP-PED AND RELAXED.

THE AIR BEING VERY HEAVY, WE HAVE THE FEELING OF "SWIMMING" THROUGH THE DENSE ATMOSPHERE AS WE MOVE IN SLOW, LEISURELY FASHION FROM BEGINNING TO END OF EACH MOVEMENT. USUALLY WE REPEAT EACH MOVEMENT 36 TIMES ON EACH SIDE.

THIS FEELING OF "SWIMMING" THROUGH VERY HEAVY AIR, WITH THE RESULTANT SURGE OF ENERGY AND TINGL-ING IN THE FINGERS, WILL EVENTUALLY BRING US THE FIRM CONVICTION THAT THIS SEEMINGLY "EMPTY" UNIVERSE IS ACTUALLY A VAST CONTINUUM OF INTELLIGENCE AND ENERGY. WHEN WE REALIZE THIS, WE HAVE REACHED A HIGH STAGE OF DEVELOPMENT. AND WHEN, ONE DAY, WE FEEL NO ONE IS DOING THE MOVEMENTS, THAT 'T'AI CHI' IS DOING 'T'AI CHI,' WE HAVE APPROACHED MASTERSHIP. IT IS AN ECSTATIC FEELING. AT SUCH TIME THE ENERGY AP-PEARS TO BE FLOWING AND WE ARE JUST SHAPING IT.

IN THE BEGINNING WE ARE APT TO FOCUS TOO MUCH ON THE HANDS, WHILE, IN TRUTH, IT IS THE LEGS WHICH ARE "YINNING AND YANGING." IT IS VITAL THAT WE BEND THE KNEES AND SHIFT OUR WEIGHT FROM THE LEFT TO

RIGHT AND BACK AGAIN. UNLIKE T'AI CHI CH'UAN, IN MANY
MOVEMENTS OF 'T'AI CHI CHIH' THE BACK HEEL COMES
OFF THE GROUND AS WE GO FORWARD AND THE FRONT
TOE LIFTS OFF THE GROUND AS THE WEIGHT SETTLES
BACK. AT ALL TIMES THE TORSO, FROM THE WAIST UP, IS
HELD RAMROD STRAIGHT, NO MATTER HOW MUCH THE
KNEES BEND (ALMOST LIKE A FENCER'S POSE, IT MIGHT
SEEM). IMPORTANT! THE HEAD AND TORSO ARE HELD IN
ERECT POSITION IN MOST MOVEMENTS, WITH THE HEAD UP
STRAIGHT AS THOUGH SUSPENDED FROM THE CEILING BY
WIRES.

AFTER WE HAVE PRACTISED 'T'AI CHI CHIH' FOR SOME
TIME, WE CAN INCREASE THE FLOW OF OUR VITAL FORCE
BY IMAGINING ALL THE ENERGY OF THE UNIVERSE COMING
IN THROUGH OUR EXTENDED FINGERS AS WE MOVE. THE
TIBETANS—AND NORTHERN INDIANS—SAY THERE ARE FIVE
COLORED PRANAS (ENERGIES), AND SEEING THESE FLOW
INDIVIDUALLY INTO THE TIPS OF THE FINGERS WILL
HEIGHTEN THE ELECTRIC FEELING, BUT THIS SHOULD NOT
BE ATTEMPTED IN THE BEGINNING. AFTER PRACTICING 'T'AI
CHI CHIH' FOR SOME YEARS, THE STUDENT MAY NOTICE A
SLIGHT TREMBLING IN HIS FINGERS AS HE PERFORMS. CER-
TAINLY HE IS NOT NERVOUS! THIS IS A FAVORABLE SIGN
THAT THE INTRINSIC ENERGY IS FLOWING SMOOTHLY
THROUGH THE MERIDIAN CHANNELS, AND IT MEANS THAT
THE PRACTISER HAS REACHED AN ADVANCED STAGE OF
DEVELOPMENT.

IN 'T'AI CHI CHIH,' MOST MOVEMENTS ARE CIRCULAR.
SOMETIMES THERE ARE SUBTLE CIRCLES WITHIN CIRCLES.
AS, WHEN WE PUSH FORWARD, WE DIP OUR ARMS SLIGHT-
LY AND THEN BRING THEM UP AGAIN, MAKING AN IM-
PERCEPTIBLE CIRCULAR MOVEMENT DOWN TO THE FLOOR.
THIS CIRCULARITY IS ONE OF THE SECRETS OF THE ENERGY
GENERATED, AND IS PART OF THE "CONTINUITY" I SO
OFTEN SPEAK OF. SINCE THE ESSENTIAL FEELING IS CIR-
CULAR, WE KEEP OUR HANDS JUST SLIGHTLY CUPPED, AS
THOUGH AROUND THE SIDES OF A BALL. WHEN WE PUSH

FORWARD (AS IN THE MOVEMENT CALLED "PUSH-PULL"),
WE DIP THE HANDS SLIGHTLY SO THERE IS A GENTLE ARC ⌣ .
THUS WE MAKE SMALL CIRCLES, AND SOMETIMES THERE
ARE CIRCLE WITHIN CIRCLES.

UNLIKE T'AI CHI CH'UAN, WHERE WE HAVE TO LEARN
AND MASTER ALL MOVEMENTS AND MEMORIZE THE ENTIRE
16-18 MINUTE SEQUENCE OF 108 MOVEMENTS (SOME ARE
REPETITIONS), IN "T'AI CHI CHIH" WE ONLY HAVE TO LEARN
5 OR 6 OF THE MOVEMENTS IN THIS BOOK AND DO THEM
REGULARLY (PERHAPS TWENTY MINUTES IN THE MORNING
AND TEN MINUTES LATER IN THE DAY), 18 TIMES ON BOTH
RIGHT AND LEFT SIDES, TO GAIN THE BENEFIT. THERE ARE
SOME MOVEMENTS, VERY POWERFUL, WE HAVE SUG-
GESTED YOU ONLY DO 9 TIMES ON EACH SIDE. SO THERE IS
NOT MUCH TO LEARN. IT IS APPLICATION—CONSTANT DAILY
PRACTISE—THAT GETS RESULTS.

THE PRACTISER MAY CHOOSE WHATEVER MOVEMENTS
APPEAL TO HIM AND SEEM TO CIRCULATE THE MOST 'CHI'
FOR HIM (NOTE THE TINGLING IN THE FINGERS AND
HANDS). A TYPICAL PROGRAM, BEGINNING WITH THE
"ROCKING MOTION" AND "BIRD FLAPS ITS WINGS," WOULD
GO ON TO ENCOMPASS "ROUND THE PLATTER" (PERHAPS
18 TIMES ON EACH SIDE), "BASS DRUM" (ALSO 18 TIMES),
"DAUGHTER ON THE MOUNTAIN TOP" AND "DAUGHTER IN
THE VALLEY" (18 TIMES), AND TWO OF THE "PULLING TAFFY
VARIATION" (3 TIMES EACH). YOU MIGHT CLOSE WITH
"PASSING CLOUDS" (9 TIMES) AND THE "SIX HEALING
SOUNDS," FOLLOWED BY THE STATIONARY "COSMIC CON-
SCIOUSNESS POSE," HELD 3-5 MINUTES.

HOWEVER, THE READER WILL PROBABLY WANT TO
MAKE HIS OWN PROGRAM, DOING THE MOVEMENTS THAT
APPEAL TO HIM MOST. TRY TO DO AT LEAST 25-30 MINUTES
A DAY, WITH PARTICULAR EMPHASIS ON DOING TCC IM-
MEDIATELY UPON ARISING. ONCE YOU GET IN THE HABIT OF
BEGINNING THE DAY THIS WAY, YOU WILL ALMOST SURELY
MISS IT IF YOU HAVE TO SKIP ONE DAY. AND NOTICE THE
SALUTARY EFFECT SUCH PRACTISE HAS ON THE REGULARI-

TY OF THE BOWELS! TCC IS ONE OF THE FEW WAYS TO EX-
ERCISE THE INTERNAL ORGANS.

IF THERE IS SUFFICIENT TIME, IT IS, OF COURSE,
BENEFICIAL TO DO ALL THE 20 MOVEMENTS. THERE IS NO
PARTICULAR EFFORT INVOLVED IN THE MOVEMENTS, SO
FATIGUE SHOULD NOT BE A FACTOR. ACTUALLY, IT SEEMS
AS IF ONE HAS MORE ENERGY AT THE FINISH OF THE PRAC-
TISE PERIOD THAN HE OR SHE HAD AT THE BEGINNING.

STANDING IN THE "COSMIC CONSCIOUSNESS POSE"
FOR A WHILE AFTER FINISHING THE MOVEMENTS WILL
BRING ONE TO A PERIOD OF REST IN WHICH THE YIN AND
YANG CHI, WHICH SEPARATED WHILE THE PRACTISER WAS
IN MOTION, HAVE A CHANCE TO FLOW TOGETHER AGAIN
AND BECOME INTEGRATED AND BALANCED. THE CHINESE
SPEAK OF "FUNCTION" WHEN THE INTRINSIC ENERGY IS IN
MOTION, THE YIN AND YANG SEPARATING. THEY ALSO
SPEAK OF "ESSENCE" WHEN THE YIN AND YANG FLOW
TOGETHER AGAIN AND THERE IS AN INNER STILLNESS. FOR
FULL INTEGRATION OF MIND AND BODY, IT IS BEST TO
PRACTISE BOTH "FUNCTION" AND "ESSENCE," OR MOVE-
MENT FOLLOWED BY STILLNESS. THE COSMIC CON-
SCIOUSNESS POSE WILL HELP EFFECT THIS BALANCE, AND
THE MEDITATION INSTRUCTION ("GREAT CIRCLE MEDITA-
TION") AT THE END OF THE BOOK CAN ALSO HELP ONE
ACHIEVE REINTEGRATION AFTER THE MOVEMENTS ARE
STILLED. THESE ARE IMPORTANT SECRETS, AND IT IS UP TO
THE READER TO AVAIL HIMSELF OF THEM AS HE WISHES.

T'AI CHI CHIH MOTIONS CAN BE PERFORMED AT ANY
SPEED. GENERALLY SPEAKING, SLOW, GENTLE MOVEMENTS
WILL STIR UP AND CIRCULATE THE MOST 'CHI,' AND THE
LEISURELY PACE WILL ENABLE THE PRACTISER TO BEND
HIS KNEES AND SHIFT HIS WEIGHT WITHOUT DIFFICULTY.
HOWEVER, THE PRACTISER SHOULD EXPERIMENT WITH DIF-
FERENT SPEEDS AND CHOOSE WHATEVER SEEMS MOST EF-
FECTIVE TO HIM.

THIS BUSINESS OF BENDING THE KNEES IS MOST
IMPORTANT. IT IS THE YINNING AND THE YANGING—

BENDING OF KNEES AND SHIFTING WEIGHT, SO FIRST ONE LEG IS "SUBSTANTIAL" AND THEN THE OTHER—THAT GREATLY ENHANCES THE FLOW OF ENERGY. DON'T TRY TO DO T'AI CHI CHIH STIFF-LEGGED! THERE SHOULD BE A GENTLE ROCKING MOTION IN THE FORWARD-AND-BACK LEG MOTIONS. THE MOTIONS ARE EASY AND NATURAL. IN THE SIDEWAYS, "T'AI CHI" STEP, USED IN SUCH MOVEMENTS AS "CARRY THE BALL TO THE SIDE" AND "PULLING TAFFY," THE LEG MUST BE SLIGHTLY BENT AND THE HEEL TOUCH THE GROUND BEFORE THE FOOT FLATTENS. DO NOT JUST FALL SIDEWAYS, BUT LIFT THE LEG SLIGHTLY, BEND THE KNEE, AND BRING THE HEEL DOWN FIRST.

MOST BEGINNERS DO NOT USE THE WRISTS AND HANDS ENOUGH, PREFERRING TO MAKE CUMBERSOME ARM MOVEMENTS. ACTUALLY, MOST OF THE T'AI CHI CHIH MOVEMENTS ARE PERFORMED WITH THE WRISTS, WHICH ARE KEPT LOOSE AND PLIABLE. FINGERS ARE SLIGHTLY SPREAD APART, THE HANDS SLIGHTLY CUPPED, AND THERE IS COMPLETE RELAXATION FROM THE WAIST UP. CONVERSELY, THE FOOT THAT IS FLAT ON THE FLOOR IS FIRM, AS THOUGH GRIPPING THE GROUND WITH THE SOLE OF THE FOOT.

MY T'AI CHI CH'UAN MASTER USED TO SAY: "TRY TO HAVE NO EXTRANEOUS THOUGHTS WHILE PRACTISING." IN OTHER WORDS, PUT YOUR CONCENTRATION IN THE SOLES OF THE FEET OR BELOW THE NAVEL (WHICHEVER IS EASIER), AND, IF POSSIBLE, KEEP IT THERE. EMPTY THE MIND BEFORE BEGINNING; FORGET TROUBLES AND OTHER PREOCCUPATION. THE GREAT CHINESE PHILOSOPHER, CHUANG TZU, SPOKE OF THE "FASTING MIND." WE KEEP OUR HEADS TOO CLUTTERED AND ACCUMULATE TOO MUCH TENSION; LET THE MIND FAST A BIT FOR 15 MINUTES!

I HAVE CHOSEN PRACTICAL, RATHER THAN POETIC, NAMES FOR THE DIFFERENT MOVEMENTS. WHEN WE SPEAK OF "AROUND THE PLATTER," IT IS NOT DIFFICULT TO ENVISION THE HANDS MOVING IN A CIRCULAR MANNER. LIKEWISE, "PUSH-PULL" IS VERY GRAPHIC, IF NOT PAR-

TICULARLY ELEGANT. THE PURPOSE OF THE NAMES IS TO
CLEARLY IDENTIFY THE MOVEMENTS AND HELP YOU
REMEMBER THEM.

   GIVE YOURSELF TO T'AI CHI CHIH FOR 30 MINUTES
EACH DAY. PRACTISE REGULARLY. THE CHINESE SAY: "YOU
CANNOT APPEASE THE HUNGER BY READING THE MENU!" IT
IS ONLY THROUGH PRACTISE THAT YOU GET RICH
REWARDS. IT IS MY FEELING THAT THE CIRCULATION OF
THE 'CHI' IS ONE OF LIFE'S GREAT SECRETS. SO, MASTER
THE SIMPLE MOVEMENTS AND PRACTISE THEM REGULARLY.
GOOD LUCK!

PART TWO

INSTRUCTION

THE FIRST TWO MOVEMENTS ARE CALLED "ROCKING MOTION" AND "BIRD FLAPS ITS WINGS." THE GENTLY UNDULATING "ROCKING MOTION" IS VAGUELY DERIVED FROM A PRACTISE THAT OLD PEOPLE IN TAIWAN AND CHINA HAVE FREQUENTLY PERFORMED, SOMETIMES AS MUCH AS 2000 TIMES A DAY. IT IS AN EXCELLENT PRELIMINARY MOVEMENT AS IT REALLY STARTS THE CIRCULATION GOING. THE ORIGINAL MOVEMENT THE OLD PEOPLE DID WAS SOMEWHAT MORE RESTRICTED AND HAS BEEN CALLED THE "DHARMA TENDON-BUILDING" MOTION, PROBABLY POINTING TO A BUDDHIST ORIGIN. I REMEMBER, ONE TIME, RECOMMENDING THAT A MAN WHO HAD SUFFERED A STROKE DO NOTHING BUT "ROCKING MOTION," AS I HAVE EVOLVED IT, WITHOUT WORRYING ABOUT TRYING TO EXECUTE THE OTHER MOVEMENTS IN THIS BOOK. HE WAS TOLD TO DO IT 1000 TIMES A DAY AND FOUND IT TO BE VERY BENEFICIAL.

THE MOVEMENT ITSELF IS RELAXING AND REFRESHING, AND, IF ONE REMEMBERS THAT THE AIR IS "VERY HEAVY" AS HIS ARMS SWING FORWARD (PALMS UP), AND THEN SWING BACK AGAIN (PALMS DOWN), HE SHOULD BEGIN TO FEEL A TINGLING IN THE FINGERS AS THE 'CHI' BEGINS TO CIRCULATE.

"BIRD FLAPS ITS WINGS" WAS A LATE-COMER, NOT APPEARING IN THE ORIGINAL EDITION OF THE BOOK. I ORIGINATED IT AFTER THE FIRST TCC LESSONS HAD BEEN GIVEN IN 1974, AND SUBSEQUENT PRACTISE FOUND IT TO BE A VERY BENEFICIAL MOVEMENT, WITH SLIGHTLY DIFFERENT EFFECTS THAN APPEAR IN OTHER MOTIONS. THIS IS NOT SURPRISING AS EACH SET OF MOVEMENTS SEEMS TO HAVE A SLIGHTLY DIFFERENT

EFFECT, ADDING UP TO COMPLETE AND WELL-ROUNDED WHOLE AS ALL, OR MOST, OF THE MOVEMENTS ARE MASTERED AND PRACTISED REGULARLY.

"ROCKING MOTION" SHOULD BE PERFORMED EFFORT-LESSLY, FOR TWO OR THREE MINUTES, BEFORE GOING ON TO "BIRD FLAPS ITS WINGS." NO NEED TO COUNT THE NUMBER OF TIMES. WITH "BIRD FLAPS ITS WINGS," EACH GROUP OF THREE, WITH THE WRISTS REVOLVING AND THE HANDS SPINNING FORWARD AND AROUND ONCE ON THE THIRD TIME, MAKES ONE COMPLETE SET. THIS SET OF THREE CAN BE REPEATED 6 OR 9 TIMES—OR MORE, IF DESIRED—AS PART OF THE MORNING ROUTINE. ONE CAN THINK OF "ROCKING MOTION" AND "BIRD FLAPS ITS WINGS" AS "PRELIMINARY" OR WARM-UP MOVEMENTS, BEFORE GOING ON TO THE MAIN BODY OF MOVEMENTS THAT BEGINS WITH "AROUND THE PLATTER."

IN THE FOLLOWING MOVES, THERE ARE BASICALLY TWO LEG MOTIONS. FIRST WE HAVE THE FORWARD AND BACK MOTION, ON THE LEFT AND ON THE RIGHT, WITH THE RIGHT HEEL COMING OFF THE GROUND AND THEN THE LEFT TOE—VICE VERSA ON THE RIGHT SIDE. THE SIDEWAYS STEP, WHERE WE SLIGHTLY BEND THE KNEE, STEP TO THE SIDE, AND COME DOWN ON THE HEEL AND THEN THE SOLE OF THE FOOT, WE CALL "THE T'AI CHI STEP." MOST, BUT NOT ALL, OF THE MAIN BODY OF MOVEMENTS USE ONE OR THE OTHER OF THESE LEG MOVEMENTS, AND THE "YINN-ING" AND "YANGING" OF THE LEGS, AS WE SHIFT THE WEIGHT TO "SUBSTANTIAL" AND "INSUBSTANTIAL" (YANG AND YING), IS EXTREMELY IMPORTANT. IT IS THE LEGS THAT SHIFT, WITH THE TORSO, FROM THE WAIST UP, STRAIGHT UP AND DOWN AS THOUGH SUSPENDED FROM THE CEILING BY WIRES.

Fig. 1

Fig. 2

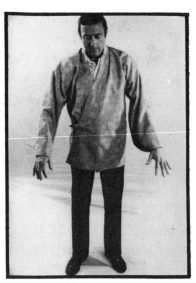

Fig. 3

Fig. 4

Fig. 5

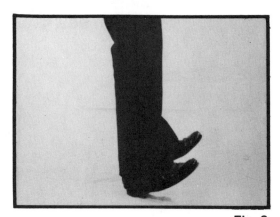

Fig. 6

THE ROCKING MOTION

STAND IN A RELAXED MANNER, FEET SLIGHTLY APART. THE ARMS ARE AT THE SIDES AND THE HANDS ARE TURNED SO THE PALMS FACE THE FRONT (SEE FIGURE I).

NOW SLOWLY ROCK FORWARD WITH THE HANDS LIFTING TO THE FRONT. AS YOU ROCK FORWARD, RISE UP ON YOUR TOES (SEE FIGURE 2).

TURN YOUR HANDS SO THE PALMS FACE DOWN AS YOU BEGIN TO LOWER THE ARMS AND YOU COME DOWN OFF YOUR TOES (SEE FIGURE 3).

AS YOU SWING DOWN, THE ARMS EXTEND TO THE BACK AND YOU NATURALLY ROCK BACK ON YOUR HEELS (FIGURE 4).

TURN YOUR PALMS TO THE FRONT (FIGURE I) AND BEGIN YOUR UPWARD SWING AGAIN (FIGURES 2, 3, 4).

NOTE: Figure 5 shows the position of the feet in Figure 2, up on the toes. Figure 6 shows the position of the feet in Figure 4, when you are back on your heels.

COMMENT: There is complete relaxation in the swings, but the air is felt to be very heavy. Fingers are spread slightly apart. 3-5 minutes of rocking should be sufficient.

Fig. 1

Fig. 2

Fig. 3

BIRD FLAPS ITS WINGS

FIGURE 1—STAND WITH FEET TOGETHER, ARMS HANGING LOOSELY IN FRONT OF YOU, PALMS FACING EACH OTHER.

FIGURE 2—FLIP WRISTS TO SIDE AND UP AS "BIRD FLAPS ITS WINGS." KNEES GO FORWARD AND TO THE SIDE IN A SLIGHTLY BOW-LEGGED POSE AS WE RISE ON THE TOES. THEN WE SLOW-LY BRING THE HANDS BACK TOGETHER, PALMS FACING EACH OTHER IN THE ORIGINAL POSI-TION, AS THE KNEES COME BACK IN AND THE LEGS STRAIGHTEN SO THAT WE ARE IN THE POSTURE OF FIGURE 1.

WE REPEAT THESE TWO MOVEMENTS.

FIGURE 3—WE AGAIN REPEAT THE "FLAPPING OF THE WINGS" AND, AS THE KNEES STAY FORWARD AND OUT

Fig. 4

Fig. 5

44

Fig. 6

FIGURE 4—WE ROTATE THE WRISTS SO THAT THE OPEN HANDS MAKE ONE CIRCLE FORWARD AND AROUND—FROM BACK, UP AND OVER AND AROUND, TO THE POSITION AT THE FINISH OF THE "FLAPPING OF THE WINGS."

FIGURE 5—WE SLOWLY BRING THE HANDS DOWN TOGETHER, PALMS FACING EACH OTHER, AS THE KNEES RETRACT AND LEGS SLIGHTLY STIFFEN, AS IN FIGURE 1.

FIGURE 6—HAVING COMPLETED ONE SERIES OF MOVEMENTS, WE NOW TURN THE HANDS DOWN, PALMS FACING THE FLOOR, AND WE PULL THE HANDS BACK TO THE SIDES IN THE FAMILIAR POSTURE OF REST.

Fig. 1

Fig. 2

46

PUT THE LEFT FOOT FORWARD AND SLIGHTLY
TO THE SIDE. AT <u>FIGURE I</u> YOU ROCK FORWARD
SO THE RIGHT HEEL LIFTS OFF THE GROUND.

AT <u>FIGURE 2</u> YOU ROCK BACK SO THE LEFT
TOE COMES OFF THE GROUND.

Note: It is suggested these two movements of the legs
be practised before the following T'AI CHI CHIH
motions are practised. They will be the basic leg
movements for about half of the succeeding moves
you will learn.

Fig. 1

Fig. 2

48

BASIC LEG MOVEMENTS (right side

HERE THE RIGHT FOOT IS FORWARD AND SLIGHTLY TO THE SIDE. AT <u>FIGURE I</u> ROCK FORWARD SO THE LEFT HEEL LIFTS OFF THE GROUND.

AT <u>FIGURE 2</u> ROCK BACK SO THE RIGHT TOE COMES OFF THE GROUND.

NOTE: These foot movements, left and right, will be co-ordinated with hand movements in the pages to follow.

Fig. 1

Fig. 2

Fig. 3

Fig. 4

AROUND THE PLATTER (left)

THE LEFT FOOT IS PLACED FORWARD IN THE
BASIC LEG MOVEMENT POSITION.

ELBOWS CLOSE TO SIDES, WE BEND THE WRISTS,
SPREAD FINGERS, AND BEGIN THE MOVEMENT
AT THE CHEST (FIGURE I).

MOVING IN A CIRCLE, FROM LEFT TO RIGHT,
AROUND AN IMAGINARY ROUND PLATTER, WE
SHIFT THE WEIGHT FORWARD (FIGURE 2) AS
THE LEFT KNEE BENDS AND THE RIGHT HEEL
COMES OFF THE GROUND.

AT FIGURE 3 WE BEGIN TO CIRCLE BACK ON THE
FAR SIDE OF THE PLATTER, AND THE WEIGHT
BEGINS TO SHIFT BACK. AT FIGURE 4 THE
WEIGHT HAS SHIFTED BACK TO THE RIGHT LEG,
KNEE BENT, AND THE LEFT TOES COME OFF THE
GROUND. THE HANDS ARE NOW BACK AT THE
CHEST, HAVING CIRCLED THE PLATTER.

NOTE: Hands are relaxed, no tension. The circular movement should be made slowly, and the bending of the
knees and shifting of the weight — Yinning and Yanning —
is all important.

Fig. 1

Fig. 2

Fig. 3

Fig. 4

52

AROUND THE PLATTER (right to left)

HANDS ARE HELD AT THE CHEST, WRISTS
SLIGHTLY BENT AND ELBOWS CLOSE TO SIDES.
FINGERS ARE SPREAD APART.

AT <u>FIGURE I</u> WE BEGIN TO ROCK FORWARD,
HANDS MOVING TO THE RIGHT (WE IMAGINE
A ROUND PLATTER AT OUR CHEST, AND THE
HANDS WILL MAKE A CIRCLE ROUND THE
PLATTER FROM RIGHT TO LEFT).

AT <u>FIGURE 2</u> THE HANDS ARE DIRECTLY
OPPOSITE AND THE LEFT HEEL IS OFF THE
GROUND (AS PRACTISED IN THE "BASIC LEG
MOVEMENTS" ON PAGE 7).

AT <u>FIGURE 3</u> WE HAVE CIRCLED THE PLATTER
SO THE HANDS ARE ON THE LEFT SIDE AND
THE BODY IS BEGINNING TO ROCK BACK.

AT <u>FIGURE 4</u> WE HAVE COMPLETED CIRCLING
THE PLATTER, THE HANDS ARE CLOSE TO THE
CHEST, AND THE RIGHT TOE IS OFF THE GROUND
(AS ON PAGE 7).

Fig. 1

Fig. 2

Fig. 3

Fig. 4

AROUND THE PLATTER (left to right) (Variation)

THIS MOVEMENT IS THE SAME AS "AROUND THE PLATTER" REGULAR SEEN ON THE PREVIOUS PAGES, EXCEPT FOR FIGURE 2.

AS THE HANDS MOVE FROM THE CHEST TO THE LEFT (FIGURE I TO FIGURE 2), THE TWO HANDS ARE TURNED SO THE PALMS FACE EACH OTHER.

THEN, IN FIGURE 3, AS THE HANDS ARE OUT OPPOSITE THE BODY, THE HANDS RESUME THEIR FORMER POSITION WITH THE PALMS FACING DOWN AND THE CIRCLE IS CONTINUED TO FIGURE 4, AND THEN BACK TO FIGURE I.

NOTE: The hands turning toward each other briefly, and then back, seems to increase the flow of CHI, or Intrinsic Energy.

Fig. 1

Fig. 2

Fig. 3

Fig. 4

AROUND THE PLATTER Variation (right)

THIS IS THE SAME AS "AROUND THE PLATTER" (RIGHT), EXCEPT THAT, AS WE BEGIN TO MOVE THE HANDS IN A CIRCLE TO THE RIGHT, WE TURN THE PALMS SO THEY FACE EACH OTHER (FIGURE 2). HERE THE WEIGHT HAS SHIFTED TO THE FRONT (LEGS NOT SHOWN).

THEN, AS THE HANDS CONTINUE THE CIRCLE FROM RIGHT TO LEFT, THEY FLATTEN OUT AGAIN (FIGURE 3) AND WE COMPLETE THE CIRCLE (FIGURE 4) WITH THE HANDS FACING THE GROUND.

NOTE: Turning the hands to face each other at the beginning of the movement is, itself, a circular motion and seems to increase the flow of Chi. As the hands reach the outer point of the arc (Figure 3) they are turned back to flat position.

Fig. 1

Fig. 2

Fig. 3

Fig. 4

BASS DRUM (left)

WE IMAGINE THERE IS A SMALL BASS DRUM
STRAPPED TO OUR CHEST, AND WE ARE GOING
TO MOVE THE HANDS AROUND IT IN A VERTICAL
CIRCLE MOVING TOWARD US.

AT FIGURE I THE WEIGHT IS ON THE REAR FOOT,
THE TOES OF THE LEFT FORWARD FOOT BEING
OFF THE GROUND. HANDS ARE ALMOST ONE
FOOT APART, PALMS FACING EACH OTHER.

AT FIGURE 2 THE HANDS DIP TO GO AROUND
THE BOTTOM OF THE DRUM AND THE WEIGHT
BEGINS TO SHIFT FORWARD. AT FIGURE 3 THE
HANDS ARE RISING AT THE FAR SIDE OF THE
CIRCLE (DRUM) AND THE WEIGHT IS ON THE
FRONT FOOT (KNEE BENT) WITH THE RIGHT
HEEL OFF THE GROUND.

AT FIGURE 4 WE HAVE COMPLETED THE CIRCLE,
HANDS MOVING BACK TOWARD BODY AND
WEIGHT SHIFTING BACK TO THE POSITION IN
FIGURE 1.

NOTE: Hands should be constantly kept at the same
distance apart. In Taiwan a stick somewhat like a bone
is held, so the two hands must remain equidistant apart.

Fig. 1

Fig. 2

Fig. 3

Fig. 4

BASS DRUM (right)

WE IMAGINE A SMALL BASS DRUM IS STRAPPED
TO OUR CHEST. OUR HANDS, PALMS FACING
EACH OTHER, ARE ABOUT ONE FOOT APART
IN FIGURE 1 AS OUR WEIGHT MOVES FORWARD
AND BOTH HANDS BEGIN TO CIRCLE THE OUTSIDE
OF THE DRUM IN A MOVEMENT UP AND AROUND
TOWARD THE BODY (FROM OUTSIDE IN).

IN FIGURE 2 WE ARE MOVING THE HANDS UP TO
THE TOP OF THE DRUM AS OUR WEIGHT GOES
FULLY FORWARD AND THE LEFT HEEL LIFTS
OFF THE GROUND.

IN FIGURE 3 WE ARE AT THE TOP OF THE DRUM
AS THE WEIGHT BEGINS TO SHIFT BACK, AND,
IN FIGURE 4 THE HANDS HAVE COME OVER THE
TOP OF THE DRUM TO THE BODY (VERY CLOSE)
AS THEY START DOWN THE INSIDE OF THE
DRUM. THE WEIGHT IS NOW BACK ON THE LEFT
FOOT AND THE RIGHT TOES ARE OFF THE
GROUND.

Fig. 3

Fig. 4

Fig. 1

Fig. 2

DAUGHTER ON THE MOUNTAINTOP (left)

WE PLACE LEFT FOOT FORWARD AND SLIGHTLY
TO SIDE, AS IN BASIC LEG MOVEMENTS.

AT FIGURE 1, WEIGHT IS BACK ON RIGHT FOOT
AND LEFT TOES ARE OFF GROUND. AS WE SHIFT
FORWARD IN FIGURE 2 (LEFT FOOT FLATTENS
AND LEFT KNEE BENDS), THE HANDS START UP
IN WIDE CIRCULAR MOTIONS.

IN FIGURE 3, AT THE TOP OF THE CIRCLES, THE
TWO PALMS COME BY EACH OTHER AND THE
WEIGHT HAS SHIFTED FORWARD SO THE RIGHT
HEEL IS OFF THE GROUND.

IN FIGURE 4, WE ARE STARTING DOWN ON THE
CIRCULAR MOTIONS, THE PALMS HAVE PASSED
EACH OTHER, AND THE WEIGHT IS BEGINNING
TO SHIFT BACK. AS THE HANDS CIRCLE AND
SEPARATE, WE COME BACK TO THE POSITION
IN FIGURE 1.

NOTE: As the hands pass each other, beginning in Figure
3, the right hand is outside the left.

Fig. 1

Fig. 2

Fig. 3

Fig. 4

64

DAUGHTER ON THE MOUNTAIN TOP (right)

THIS IS THE SAME AS THE TWO PREVIOUS PAGES, ONLY TO THE RIGHT SIDE.

IN FIGURES 1 AND 2, THE HANDS ARE BEGINNING TO RISE ON THE OUTSIDE OF THEIR CIRCLES, AND THE WEIGHT STARTS TO SHIFT FORWARD.

IN FIGURE 3, THE WEIGHT HAS SHIFTED FORWARD TO THE RIGHT FOOT AND THE LEFT HEEL IS OFF THE GROUND, AS THE HANDS CROSS WITH THE RIGHT HAND ON THE OUTSIDE.

AT FIGURE 4, THE HANDS HAVE CROSSED AND ARE BEGINNING TO DESCEND ON THE INSIDE OF THE OVAL—SHAPED CIRCLES AS THE WEIGHT STARTS TO SHIFT BACK TO THE POSITION IN FIGURE 1.

NOTE: It is suggested "Daughter on the Mountaintop" be done 18 or 36 times on the left and 18 or 36 times on the right.

Fig. 1

Fig. 2

Fig. 3

Fig. 4

66

DAUGHTER IN THE VALLEY (left)

THIS MOVEMENT IS ALMOST THE OPPOSITE OF "DAUGHTER ON THE MOUNTAINTOP" AS WE SCOOP UNDERHAND INSTEAD OF CURVING OVERHAND OVER THE TOPS OF THE OVALS.

AT FIGURE 1, WEIGHT IS ON BACK FOOT, LEFT TOES IN AIR. THE HANDS MOVE SLIGHTLY DOWNWARD IN FIGURE 2 IN A SCOOPING MOTION AS WEIGHT BEGINS TO SHIFT FORWARD.

IN FIGURE 3, WE ARE AT THE TOP OF THE SCOOP. THE TWO OPEN PALMS COME TOGETHER WITHOUT TOUCHING, AND THE WEIGHT HAS SHIFTED FORWARD TO THE BENT LEFT KNEE AS THE RIGHT HEEL LIFTS OFF THE GROUND.

AT FIGURE 4, THE HANDS SEPARATE AS THEY CONTINUE THEIR OVAL MOVEMENTS, AND THE WEIGHT BEGINS TO SHIFT BACK TO THE POSITION IN FIGURE 1.

NOTE: Although the air is felt as heavy, there is no tension in the hands or arms, which are relaxed.

Fig. 1

Fig. 2

Fig. 3

Fig. 4

68

DAUGHTER IN THE VALLEY (right)

THIS IS THE SAME AS "DAUGHTER IN THE VALLEY", LEFT SIDE, ONLY WE MOVE FORWARD AND TO THE RIGHT.

AT FIGURE 1, WITH WEIGHT BACK, THE HANDS BEGIN THEIR DOWNWARD SCOOPING MOTION, CONTINUING IN FIGURE 2 AND COMING TO THE APEX, PALMS ALMOST TOUCHING, AS WEIGHT SHIFTS FORWARD IN FIGURE 3.

AT FIGURE 4 THE HANDS HAVE SEPARATED AS THEY START THEIR DOWNWARD ARCS AND THE WEIGHT HAS BEGUN TO SHIFT BACK.

NOTE: It is suggested this movement be performed 18 or 36 times in a completely relaxed fashion. Be sure the weight shifts as indicated.

CARRY BALL TO LEFT (three times)

AT <u>FIGURE 1</u> WE SLIGHTLY CUP HANDS, AS THOUGH HOLDING A BALL. THE TWO FEET ARE PARALLEL, AND THE WEIGHT IS SLIGHTLY ON THE RIGHT FOOT.

AT <u>FIGURE 2</u> THE WEIGHT BEGINS TO SHIFT TO LEFT AND THE HANDS GO DOWN IN A CIRCULAR MOTION, COMING AROUND THE BOTTOM OF THE CIRCLE.

AT <u>FIGURE 3</u> THE HANDS, STILL CARRYING THE BALL (PALMS FACING EACH OTHER) ARE RISING ON THE OUTSIDE OF THE CIRCLE, AND THE WEIGHT IS ON THE LEFT FOOT (BOTH FEET ARE KEPT ALMOST FLAT ON THE GROUND).

AT <u>FIGURE 4</u> WE BRING THE BALL TO THE TOP OF THE CIRCLE, AS THE WEIGHT SHIFTS BACK.

NOTE: We do this movement three (3) times to the left, then do "Carry Ball to Right" (following pages) three (3) times to the right. This makes one full movement. We suggest the whole (6 moves) 3 or 9 times.

Fig. 3   Fig. 4

Fig. 1   Fig. 2

CARRY BALL TO RIGHT

AT FIGURE 1 BALL IS HELD AT LEFT SHOULDER, HANDS SLIGHTLY CUPPED AND WEIGHT MOSTLY ON LEFT FOOT (WHICH IS PARALLEL TO RIGHT).

AT FIGURE 2 HANDS CARRY THE BALL (PALMS FACING EACH OTHER) DOWN IN CIRCULAR MOVE AS WEIGHT SHIFTS TO RIGHT.

AT FIGURE 3 HANDS ARE RISING AT FAR SIDE OF CIRCLE, REACHING THE TOP OF THE CIRCLE AT FIGURE 4 AS THE WEIGHT BEGINS TO SHIFT BACK TO THE LEFT.

NOTE: Three times to the left, then three times to the right make up one complete movement. Use the hands and wrists more than the arms in carrying the ball.

Fig. 1

Fig. 2

Fig. 3

Fig. 4

Fig. 1

Fig. 2

Fig. 3

Fig. 4

PUSH PULL (left)

BEND WRISTS AND PLACE HANDS, FINGERS SPREAD, IN FRONT OF SHOULDERS. WEIGHT IS ON THE BACK FOOT, KNEE BENT. LEFT FRONT FOOT HAS TOES SLIGHTLY OFF GROUND (FIGURE 1).

PUSH HANDS OUT FROM CHEST, DIPPING SLIGHTLY (THE AIR IS FELT AS VERY HEAVY). WEIGHT SHIFTS FORWARD TO LEFT FOOT AS TOES COME DOWN FLAT. RIGHT HEEL LIFTS OFF GROUND (FIGURE 2).

TURN HANDS OVER SO PALMS FACE UP AND BEGIN TO PULL BACK (FIGURE 3).

AS HANDS, PALMS UP, APPROACH CHEST, WEIGHT SHIFTS TO FLATTENED BACK FOOT AND LEFT TOES BEGIN TO LIFT OFF GROUND (FIGURE 4). FROM HERE WE TURN HANDS AND BEGIN AGAIN AT FIGURE 1.

NOTE: We concentrate on the right hand (60%) as we push, so it will be positive to balance the left 'substantial' (or YANG) leg.

Fig. 1

Fig. 2

Fig. 3

Fig. 4

PUSH PULL (right)

HANDS AT SHOULDERS, WRISTS SLIGHTLY BENT,
RIGHT FOOT FORWARD (FIGURE 1), PUSH FORWARD
AND SHIFT WEIGHT (FIGURE 2).

AT FIGURE 3, LEFT HEEL IS OFF GROUND. WE
TURN HANDS OVER AND, AT FIGURE 4, HAVE
PULLED HANDS BACK TOWARD SHOULDERS AS
WEIGHT SHIFTS BACK. THEN WE CONTINUE FROM
FIGURE 1, TURNING HANDS TO FRONT.

NOTE: With right leg forward, we concentrate on the
left hand (60%) as we push forward.

Fig. 1

Fig. 2

Fig. 3

Fig. 4

PULLING IN THE ENERGY (left)

WE TURN THE HANDS SO THE PALMS FACE UP, FINGERS SPREAD APART. FROM FIGURE 1, WHERE THE WEIGHT IS ON THE BACK FOOT AND THE LEFT TOES ARE OFF THE GROUND, WE SHIFT THE WEIGHT FORWARD AS THE HANDS BEGIN TO MOVE IN A CIRCLE, LEFT TO RIGHT, (THE SAME AS "AROUND THE PLATTER", ONLY PALMS FACE UP) IN FIGURE 2.

AT FIGURE 3 HANDS ARE MIDWAY IN THE CIRCULAR MOTION AND WEIGHT IS SHIFTED FORWARD SO RIGHT HEEL IS OFF GROUND. AT FIGURE 4 WE ARE COMPLETING THE CIRCLE AND THE WEIGHT IS BEGINNING TO SHIFT BACK TO THE RIGHT FOOT SO WE CAN START AGAIN AT FIGURE 1.

NOTE: The flow of CHI can be greatly increased by imagining all the Energy of the Universe flowing in thru the fingers. INDIAN sages speak of "five colored Pranas (or Universal Energies)". If we can imagine these five colored energies coming in thru the fingers, the effect should be strong.

COMMENT: As this is a very powerful movement, we only do it 3 or 9 times on each side.

Fig. 1

Fig. 2

Fig. 3

Fig. 4

PULLING IN THE ENERGY (right)

THE SAME AS THE PREVIOUS MOVEMENT, ONLY, THIS TIME, WE MOVE RIGHT TO LEFT.

AT FIGURE 1 THE WEIGHT IS BACK. WE START THE CIRCLE TO THE RIGHT AT FIGURE 2 AND WEIGHT BEGINS TO SHIFT FORWARD.

AT FIGURE 3 THE HANDS ARE EXTENDED FROM BODY, WEIGHT IS FORWARD, AND LEFT HEEL OFF GROUND. AT FIGURE 4 THE WEIGHT IS BEGINNING TO SHIFT BACK AND CIRCLE IS BEING COMPLETED, LEADING TO FIGURE 1 AGAIN.

NOTE: First practise the movements alone, then begin to imagine the energies (Pranas) coming in thru the fingers.

Fig. 1

Fig. 3

Fig. 2

Fig. 4

PULLING TAFFY (left)

WE BEGIN (FIGURE 1) WITH HANDS AT SIDES,
PALMS DOWN, AND KNEES SLIGHTLY BENT.

IN FIGURE 2 THE HANDS HAVE RISEN SO THE
RIGHT PALM IS SLIGHTLY CUPPED OVER THE
LEFT PALM, THE ELBOWS EXTENDED FROM
THE SIDES AND THE WEIGHT ON THE RIGHT
LEG AS WE RAISE THE LEFT TOES AND LIGHTLY
BALANCE ON THE LEFT HEEL.

IN FIGURE 3 WE HAVE PULLED THE HANDS
APART, AS THOUGH STRETCHING STICKY TAFFY.
THE RIGHT HAND PUSHES DOWN ALONG THE
RIGHT LEG, AND WE CONCENTRATE ON THE
RIGHT HAND.

IN FIGURE 4 THE HANDS HAVE NATURALLY
CIRCLED BACK TO THE SIDES, PALMS DOWN,
IN A POSITION LIKE THAT OF FIGURE 1.

NOTE: Really pull the sticky taffy apart! Push down
with the right hand.

Fig. 1

Fig. 2

Fig. 3

Fig. 4

PULLING TAFFY (right)

WE BEGIN (FIGURE 1) WITH HANDS AT SIDES, PALMS DOWN, AND KNEES SLIGHTLY BENT.

THE HANDS RISE AND, IN FIGURE 2, THE LEFT HAND IS SLIGHTLY ABOVE THE RIGHT, PALMS FACING EACH OTHER. THE ELBOWS ARE EXTENDED AWAY FROM THE SIDES, AND THE RIGHT TOE IS SLIGHTLY RAISED SO WE REST ON THE RIGHT HEEL.

IN FIGURE 3 THE HANDS HAVE PULLED APART, AS THOUGH THEY ARE STRETCHING VERY STICKY TAFFY. THE LEFT HAND GOES DOWN ALONG THE LEFT LEG, FLAT TO THE GROUND, AND WE CONCENTRATE ON THE LEFT, NOT THE RIGHT, HAND.

IN FIGURE 4 WE HAVE TURNED BACK TOWARD THE FRONT AND THE HANDS COME DOWN TO THE SIDES, SIMILAR TO FIGURE 1.

NOTE: Concentrating on the left hand (to balance the 'substantial' right leg) and really pulling the palms past each other is important.

Fig. 1

Fig. 2

Fig. 3

Fig. 4

Fig. 5

Fig. 6

PULLING TAFFY (left) (Variation 'A')—front and side

IN THIS VARIATION WE "PULL TAFFY" FORWARD
AND SLIGHTLY TO THE SIDE (SEE FIGURES 1 AND 2).

AT FIGURE 3, WE ARE PULLING BACK THE HANDS
AND SHIFTING OUR WEIGHT TO NEUTRAL. AT
FIGURE 4 THE HANDS HAVE DROPPED TO THE SIDES
AND FEET ARE ALMOST TOGETHER.

THEN, IN FIGURES 5 AND 6 WE DO THE REGULAR
"PULLING TAFFY" TO THE LEFT.

NOTE: As we move forward and slightly to the left in
Figures 1 and 2, we first touch the left heel to the ground
and then bring the weight forward as the left foot flattens
out.

COMMENT: We are imposing two "pulling taffy" movements,
one forward and one sideward, on each other — they are
consecutive. We suggest this be done 9 or 18 times.

Fig. 1

Fig. 2

Fig. 3

Fig. 4

Fig. 5

Fig. 6

PULLING TAFFY (right) (Variation 'A')—front and side

ON THE PREVIOUS TWO PAGES WE MOVED FRONT
AND SIDE TO THE LEFT. NOW WE REVERSE AND
DO THIS VARIATION TO THE RIGHT.

IN FIGURES 1 AND 2 WE PULL TO THE FRONT
(AND SLIGHTLY TO THE RIGHT), WEIGHT SHIFTING
FORWARD TO THE BENT RIGHT KNEE.

IN FIGURES 3 AND 4 WE SHIFT BACK TO NEUTRAL,
HANDS COMING TO REST AT THE SIDES.

IN FIGURES 5 AND 6 WE DO THE FAMILIAR
"PULLING TAFFY" TO THE RIGHT SIDE.

Fig. 1

Fig. 2

Fig. 3

Fig. 4

Fig. 5

Fig. 6

PULLING TAFFY (left) (Variation 'B')

STANDING WITH THE FEET SLIGHTLY APART, WE
ROTATE THE HANDS THREE TIMES FROM BOTTOM
TO TOP (USING THE WRIST, NOT THE ARM),
BEGINNING AS AT FIGURE 1.

IN FIGURES 2 AND 3 WE ARE ROTATING, DOWN
AND AROUND, AND AT FIGURE 4 THE HANDS ARE
RISING. AT THE TOP OF THE THIRD CIRCULAR
MOTION WE MOVE TO THE FAMILIAR "PULLING
TAFFY" POSITION IN FIGURE 5, AND WE PULL
THE HANDS APART (RIGHT HAND GOING DOWN
THE LEG) AT FIGURE 6.

NOTE: After doing this once to the left (three rotations
of hands and then "pulling taffy"), we can do it once to
the right, as seen on page 29. Alternating left, then right,
it is suggested we do the movement 9 or 18 times on each
side.

Fig. 1

Fig. 2

Fig. 3

Fig. 4

Fig. 5

Fig. 6

92

PULLING TAFFY (right) (Variation 'B')

WE BEGIN THE SAME AS WE DID ON THE PREVIOUS
PAGES, FEET APART AND HANDS MAKING RELAXED
CIRCLE (DOWN, AROUND, AND UP) THREE TIMES —
AS IN FIGURES 1, 2, 3 AND 4, BEFORE MOVING THE
HANDS FROM THE TOP OF THE LOOP TO THE
POSITION IN FIGURE 5, AND THEN IN FIGURE 6.

NOTE: Fingers are spread apart. The loops are made only
by the hands from the wrist, then the elbows extend from
the sides as we "pull taffy" in Figures 5 and 6.

Fig. 1

Fig. 2

Fig. 3

Fig. 4

94

Fig. 5

Fig. 6

Fig. 7   Fig. 8

PULLING TAFFY (Variation 'C') (Perpetual Motion Variation)

THIS VARIATION BEGINS THE SAME AS REGULAR
"PULLING TAFFY" (FIGURES 1 AND 2). IN FIGURE 3
THE WAIST PIVOTS TO THE LEFT AND THE LEFT
HAND RISES IN A CIRCLE (FEET DO NOT MOVE).

IN FIGURE 4 WE HOLD A BALL ON THE LEFT SIDE,
AND THEN THE HANDS ALMOST COME TOGETHER,
LEFT HAND STILL ON TOP, IN FIGURE 5. WE
CONTINUE THE REGULAR "PULLING TAFFY" MOVE
IN FIGURE 6.

IN FIGURE 7 THE WAIST HAS TURNED TO THE RIGHT,
FEET STILL FLAT ON THE GROUND, AND NOW THE
RIGHT HAND HAS RISEN IN A CIRCLE TO THE POINT
WHERE WE ARE HOLDING A BALL (IN FIGURE 8)
WITH THE RIGHT HAND ON TOP. THIS CONTINUES
BACK INTO FIGURE 1 AND WE REPEAT THE SEQUENCE.

Fig. 1

Fig. 2

Fig. 3

Fig. 4

Fig. 5

Fig. 6

WORKING THE PULLEY (left)

AT FIGURE 1 LEFT HAND IS AT SHOULDER AND
WEIGHT IS ON THE RIGHT FOOT, LEFT TOES IN
AIR. AT FIGURE 2 LEFT HAND PUSHES FORWARD
AND WEIGHT BEGINS TO SHIFT FORWARD. AT
FIGURE 3 WEIGHT IS COMPLETELY ON FRONT
FOOT AND RIGHT HEEL IS OFF GROUND. LEFT
HAND HAS ENDED PUSH FORWARD AND NOW
IS TURNING OVER, PALM UP. THE RIGHT HAND
IS AT THE SHOULDER.

AS THE RIGHT HAND BEGINS TO PUSH FORWARD
IN FIGURE 4, THE WEIGHT STARTS TO SHIFT
BACK AND THE LEFT HAND BEGINS TO SLOWLY
PULL BACK AT THE WAIST, PALM UP. IN FIGURE
5 THE WEIGHT HAS SHIFTED TO THE BACK FOOT
AND THE LEFT TOES ARE OFF THE GROUND. THE
LEFT HAND HAS PULLED BACK EVEN WITH THE
BODY AS THE RIGHT HAND PUSHES ALL THE WAY
OUT. AT FIGURE 6 THE RIGHT HAND HAS TURNED
OVER AND IS ABOUT TO PULL BACK. THE LEFT
HAND HAS CIRCLED (AS IN A SWIMMING MOTION)
AND IS NOW TURNED TO THE FRONT, READY TO
CONTINUE AS IN FIGURE 1.

NOTE: When the right hand pushes out, it is working
against the weight, which is shifting back. Do these
movements slowly for maximum results.

Fig. 1

Fig. 2

Fig. 3

Fig. 4

Fig. 5

Fig. 6

98

WORKING THE PULLEY (right)

IN FIGURES 1 AND 2 WE BEGIN TO PUSH THE
RIGHT HAND FORWARD FROM THE SHOULDER
AND SHIFT THE WEIGHT TO THE FRONT.

AT FIGURE 3 THE WEIGHT IS FULLY FORWARD
ON THE RIGHT FOOT, THE LEFT HEEL IS OFF
THE GROUND, AND THE RIGHT HAND BEGINS
TO TURN OVER SO WE CAN BEGIN THE PULL
BACK AT THE WAIST IN FIGURE 4 AS THE LEFT
HAND PUSHES OUT FROM THE SHOULDER.

AT FIGURE 5 THE LEFT HAND HAS REACHED
MAXIMUM EXTENSION AND WEIGHT IS
BEGINNING TO SHIFT BACK, SO THAT AT
FIGURE 6 THE RIGHT HAND, IN A SWIMMING
MOTION, HAS COME UP AND OVER TO THE
SHOULDER AND THE LEFT HAND HAS TURNED
PALM UP, AND IS BEGINNING TO PULL BACK
AT THE WAIST.

NOTE: Remeber that the air is very heavy, like water,
as we "swim" thru it in pulling back or pushing forward.
Be sure to shift weight.

Fig. 1

Fig. 2

Fig. 3

Fig. 4

LIGHT AT THE TOP OF THE HEAD

STAND IN A RELAXED FASHION WITH HANDS AT THE SIDES.

FIGURE 1—SLOWLY, WITHOUT ANY PRESSURE, BEGIN TO LIFT THE HANDS TOWARD THE HEAD, WITH PALMS POINTED UPWARD.

FIGURE 2—HANDS REACH A POSITION DIRECTLY ABOVE THE HEAD, PALMS FACING EACH OTHER.

FIGURE 3—"OUT"—THE HANDS MOVE ABOUT EIGHTEEN INCHES TO THE SIDES AND WE RISE UP ON OUR TOES.

FIGURE 4—"IN"—THE HANDS COME BACK TO THE POSITION OF FIGURE 2, DIRECTLY ABOVE THE HEAD, AND WE COME DOWN OFF THE TOES TO THE SOLES OF OUR FEET.

Repeat FIGURES 3 AND 4—"Out" and "In"—twice (making three "Outs" and three "Ins" altogether).

Fig. 5

Fig. 6

Fig. 7

Fig. 8

LIGHT AT THE TOP OF THE HEAD (cont'd.)

FIGURE 5—NOW, WITH HANDS DIRECTLY OVERHEAD, PALMS FACING EACH OTHER, WE "MIX"—MAKE A CIRCULAR MOTION (BACK, UP AND OVER, TO THE FRONT) WITH EACH HAND, AS THOUGH WE ARE RUBBING OUR PALMS TOGETHER, THOUGH THE PALMS ARE STILL ABOUT FOUR INCHES APART. WE DO THIS FOR ABOUT 15-20 SECONDS.

FIGURE 6—"HOLD"—WE STOP CIRCLING THE HANDS AND HOLD THEM STILL, PALMS FACING EACH OTHER, FOR ABOUT 15-20 SECONDS. NOTE THE (POSSIBLE) THROBBING SENSATION.

NOW REPEAT FIGURE 3 ("OUT") AND FIGURE 4 ("IN"), THEN REPEAT BOTH AGAIN. NOW JUST DO FIGURE 3 ("OUT") AS WE RISE ON OUR TOES, AND, FROM THIS "OUT" POSITION, WE GRADUALLY LOWER THE HANDS TO THE WAIST (COMING DOWN OFF OUR TOES) AND THEN SWOOP THE HANDS TOWARD EACH OTHER.

FIGURE 7—THE RIGHT HAND NOW PASSES UNDER THE LEFT, BOTH PALMS FACING UP. WE COMPLETE THE CIRCLES AND THE RIGHT HAND GOES TO THE RIGHT AND THE LEFT HAND TO THE LEFT.

FIGURE 8—NOW THE HANDS ARE GRADUALLY LOWERED TO THE SIDES IN THE POSITION OF REST, WITH PALMS FACING DOWN, PARALLEL TO THE FLOOR; KNEES ARE SLIGHTLY BENT.

Fig. 1

Fig. 2

Fig. 3

Fig. 4

Fig. 5

JOYOUS BREATH

NOTE: This has elements of the Aikido breathing in it, and is a good preliminary exercise.

It is the only movement in which we use force.

AT FIGURE 1 WE PUSH DOWN, DRIVING THE HEAVY AIR INTO THE GROUND. THEN WE TURN THE HANDS PALMS UP (FIGURE 2) AS THE BENT KNEES BEGIN TO STRAIGHTEN AND WE FORCIBLY LIFT THE HEAVY AIR AS WE BREATHE IN.

AT FIGURE 3 THE BREATH IS FULL, AND WE HOLD IT A COMFORTABLE PERIOD (PERHAPS 15 SECONDS), RETAINING OUR POSITION UP ON THE TOES. THEN WE BEGIN TO BREATH OUT (FIGURE 4) AS WE TURN THE HANDS OVER AND BEGIN TO PUSH THE AIR INTO THE GROUND. AT FIGURE 5 THE BREATH IS OUT AND KNEES ARE BENT.

NOTE: We suggest doing this breath 6 or 9 times as a preliminary exercise, or 3 times as part of T'ai Chi Chih, but only in an area where the air is relatively pure.

Fig. 1

Fig. 2

Fig. 3

Fig. 4

PASSING CLOUDS

NOTE: This movement is very similar to "Waving the Hands like Clouds" of T'ai Chi Chu'an, only the feet do not move, the pivoting waist causing the movement.

AT FIGURE 1 THE WAIST IS TURNED TO THE RIGHT AS THE LEFT HAND, FINGERS SPREAD, BEGINS A CIRCULAR MOTION TO CARRY IT IN FRONT OF THE FACE AT FIGURE 2, AS THE RIGHT HAND BEGINS A CIRCLE IN THE OPPOSITE DIRECTION. THE WEIGHT IS BEGINNING TO SHIFT TO THE LEFT, BUT THE FEET ARE KEPT FLAT ON THE GROUND.

AT FIGURE 3 THE RIGHT HAND IS RISING IN ITS CIRCLE AND THE WAIST IS TWISTED TO THE LEFT. THE LEFT HAND IS BEGINNING TO DROP ON THE OUTSIDE OF ITS CIRCLE, AND CONTINUES IN FIGURE 4 AS THE RIGHT HAND BEGINS TO MOVE IN FRONT OF THE FACE. RIGHT HAND WILL THEN CIRCLE DOWN AS LEFT HAND RISES, BACK TO POSITION OF FIGURE 1.

THIS SHOULD BE DONE 9 OR 18 TIMES. IF 18, THE TEMPO CAN GRADUALLY BE SPEEDED UP FROM SLOW TO FAST. BE SURE TO SWIVEL THE WAIST!

THE SIX HEALING SOUNDS

IN ANCIENT TIMES THERE WERE TWO PARTICULARLY STRONG INFLUENCES IN CHINESE LIFE. THEY WERE: CONFUCIANISM AND TAOISM.

THE TEACHINGS OF CONFUCIUS WERE MOSTLY HUMANISTIC IN CHARACTER. THEY HAD TO DO WITH CORRECT SOCIAL CONDUCT, THE ART OF GOVERNING, FILIAL PIETY, OBSERVANCE OF RITES, AND SO FORTH. AS SUCH, THEY HAVE HAD A TREMENDOUS INFLUENCE ON ASIAN CULTURE FOR 2500 YEARS, CONTINUING UNTIL THIS DAY. JAPAN IS LARGELY A CONFUCIAN COUNTRY, AND OWES MUCH TO THE SAGE'S TEACHING.

TAOISM, ON THE OTHER HAND, WAS LARGELY MYSTIC IN NATURE. IT IS USUALLY TRACED TO THE SAGE LAO-TZU, SUPPOSEDLY A CONTEMPORARY OF CONFUCIUS. THE HISTORICITY OF THIS WISE MAN IS SOMETIMES SUSPECT, BUT THERE IS NO DOUBT OF THE INFLUENCE OF THE "TAO TEH CHING" ASCRIBED TO LAO-TZU AND, ACCORDING TO LEGEND, DASHED OFF BY HIM AT THE REQUEST OF THE FRONTIER GUARD (HIMSELF AN UNUSUAL MAN) WHO WAS THE LAST TO SEE LAO-TZU BEFORE THE LATTER LEFT HIS KINGDOM AND DISAPPEARED.

THE TAO TEH CHING HAS BEEN TRANSLATED AT LEAST SIXTY OR SEVENTY TIMES INTO ENGLISH, MAKING IT PERHAPS THE MOST TRANSLATED OF ALL LITERARY WORKS, INCLUDING THE BIBLE.

THE TAOISTS, WHO WERE CLOSE TO NATURE AND

SOUGHT TO FLOW WITH THE CURRENT OF THE SUPREME
ULTIMATE (TAO, OR T'AI CHI), CARED NOT A FIG FOR
CORRECTNESS. LAO-TZU DID NOT VALUE EDUCATION,
MORALITY, AND OTHER "VIRTUES", WHICH HE SAID,
IMMEDIATELY CREATED THEIR OPPOSITES. IN THE WORLD
OF ONENESS, SUCH POLARITY DID NOT EXIST. SO, TRUE
TAOISTS, BEFORE THE TEACHINGS DEGENERATED INTO
A SECOND-RATE RELIGION, OFTEN SPENT TIME IN THE
FORESTS, OR ON MOUNTAIN TOPS, IN DEEP AND SOLITARY
MEDITATION. MANY OF THE MAGNIFICENT LANDSCAPE
SCROLLS OF CHINA SHOW THESE SHADOWY SAGES,
LOOKING RATHER SMALL IN THE OVERWHELMING SCENES
OF WATERFALLS AND ROCKY CLIFFS. SOMETIMES, IN THE
BACKGROUND, WE CAN JUST DISCERN A HERMIT'S HUT.

LIVING THIS NATURAL LIFE IN THE WILDERNESS,
THESE WISE MEN WERE, OF COURSE, EXPOSED TO HARD-
SHIPS AND DISEASE. ACCORDING TO LEGEND, THEY
EVOLVED A METHOD OF REPEATING CERTAIN SOUNDS,
SYNCHRONIZED WITH A MOTION RESEMBLING 'T'AI
CHI CHIH', IN ORDER TO WARD OFF ILLNESS OR CURE
ANY INDISPOSITION. EACH SOUND REFERRED TO A
PARTICULAR INNER ORGAN, AND THE IDEA WAS TO
CONCENTRATE ON THE APPROPRIATE ORGAN WHILE
MAKING THE MOVEMENT AND SLOWLY UTTERING THE
CORRECT SOUND IN A LONG DRAWN-OUT WHISPER.
THESE SIX SOUNDS, WITH THE ORGANS THEY SERVED
AND THE CHINESE CHARACTER FOR THE SOUNDS, ARE:

HO	(HEART)	呵
HU	(SPLEEN)	呼
SZU	(LIVER)	噓
HSU	(LUNGS)	泗

HSI   (3 HEATERS: BELOW THE NAVEL,
                                     IN THE ABDOMEN,
                                     BETWEEN THE EYES)

CHUI   (KIDNEYS)

嗜
吹

ON THE NEXT PAGE WILL BE FOUND INSTRUCTIONS
FOR MAKING THE MOVEMENT, ON BOTH LEFT AND RIGHT
SIDES, AND REPEATING THE SOUNDS. SINCE 9 IS THE
CHINESE POSITIVE NUMBER, IN PRACTICE WE SHOULD
PERFORM 9, 18, OR 36 TIMES ON EACH SIDE. IT IS ESSENTIAL
THAT THESE SOUNDS BE PRACTISED IN GOOD, PURE AIR;
NEXT TO AN OPEN WINDOW EARLY IN THE MORNING,
AFTER FINISHING 'T'AI CHIH' PRACTICE, IS AS GOOD A
TIME AS ANY.

Fig. 1

Fig. 2

Fig. 3

Fig. 4

THE SIX HEALING SOUNDS
(performed vigorously)

FIGURE 1 —STAND IN A RELAXED MANNER, HANDS AT THE CHEST, PALMS FACING FORWARD AND FINGERTIPS POINTING AT THE CEILING.

FIGURE 2 —STEP FORWARD WITH LEFT FOOT, HEEL TOUCHING THE GROUND FIRST, THEN SOLE OF THE FOOT. AT SAME TIME PUSH LEFT ARM FORWARD (WRIST COCKED BACK SLIGHTLY) AND VIGOROUSLY ASPIRATE (WHISPER LOUDLY) THE SOUND "HO!" THEN PULL LEFT ARM BACK, BUT NOT LEFT LEG.

FIGURE 3 —LIFT LEFT LEG, BEND KNEE SLIGHTLY, AND COME DOWN ON HEEL AGAIN. AT SAME TIME PUSH BOTH ARMS FORWARD FROM CHEST AND ASPIRATE THE SOUND "HU!" THEN PULL BOTH ARMS BACK.

FIGURE 4 —NOW, SWEEP HANDS FROM RIGHT TO LEFT ABOUT TWO FEET. BOTH HANDS ARE FAC-ING TO THE LEFT. THE RIGHT ELBOW IS TUCKED IN AT THE SIDE, THE LEFT ELBOW BEING UP AND OUT AT ABOUT THE LEVEL OF THE HANDS. THE LEFT LEG HAS BEEN PULLED BACK AND NOW STEPS DIRECTLY TO THE SIDE, HEEL TOUCHING FIRST. AT SAME TIME ASPIRATE THE SOUND "TZU!"

Fig. 5

Fig. 6

Fig. 7

FIGURE 5—STEP FORWARD WITH RIGHT FOOT, HEEL TOUCHING GROUND FIRST, THEN SOLE OF FOOT. AT SAME TIME PUSH RIGHT ARM FORWARD (WRIST COCKED BACK SLIGHTLY) AND ASPIRATE THE SOUND "SHUH!" THEN PULL RIGHT ARM BACK.

FIGURE 6—LIFT RIGHT LEG, BEND KNEE SLIGHTLY, AND COME DOWN ON HEEL AGAIN. AT SAME TIME PUSH <u>BOTH</u> ARMS FORWARD FROM CHEST AND ASPIRATE THE SOUND "SHEE!" THEN PULL BOTH ARMS BACK.

FIGURE 7—NOW SWEEP FROM LEFT TO RIGHT ABOUT TWO FEET. BOTH HANDS ARE FACING TO THE RIGHT. THE LEFT ELBOW IS TUCKED IN AT SIDE, THE RIGHT ELBOW BEING UP AND OUT AT ABOUT THE LEVEL OF THE HANDS. THE RIGHT LEG HAS BEEN PULLED BACK AND NOW STEPS DIRECTLY TO THE RIGHT SIDE, HEEL TOUCHING FIRST. AT SAME TIME ASPIRATE THE SOUND "CHUI!" THEN BRING HANDS BACK TO CHEST AND FEET TOGETHER IN POSE OF PANEL 1.

Fig. 8

Fig. 9

Fig. 10

Fig. 11

REPEAT LEFT AND RIGHT SIDE—DOING HO, HU, TZU, SHUH, SHEE, CHUI.

REPEAT AGAIN (THIRD TIME) ON LEFT AND RIGHT, BUT, AFTER "CHUI!" (WITH HANDS MOVING TO LEFT), FIGURE 8—TURN THE HANDS TO THE RIGHT AND SWEEP TO THE RIGHT AS YOU ASPIRATE "CHUI!" AGAIN, LIFTING THE RIGHT FOOT AND COMING DOWN ON THE HEEL.

FIGURE 9—TURN HANDS TO LEFT, LIFT LEFT LEG AND COME DOWN ON HEEL, AND SWEEP HANDS TO THE LEFT AS YOU ASPIRATE "CHUI!"

FIGURE 10—TURN HANDS TO RIGHT, LIFT RIGHT LEG AND COME DOWN ON HEEL, AND SWEEP HANDS TO RIGHT AS YOU ASPIRATE "CHUI!"

FIGURE 11—TURN HANDS TO LEFT, LIFT LEFT LEG AND COME DOWN ON HEEL AND SWEEP HANDS TO THE LEFT AS YOU ASPIRATE "CHUI!" THEN CIRCLE HANDS BACK TO CENTER AND GRADUAL-LY LOWER THEM TO SIDES, PALMS FLUSH TO AND PARALLEL WITH THE FLOOR IN THE USUAL POSI-TION OF REST.

Fig. 1

Fig. 2

COSMIC CONSCIOUSNESS POSE

THERE IS NO MOVEMENT IN THIS STANCE.
FIGURE I SHOWS A FRONT VIEW AND FIGURE 2
SHOWS A SIDE VIEW, SO IT CAN BE NOTED
THAT THE RIGHT HAND IS OUTSIDE THE LEFT
(FARTHER FROM THE BODY). JUST THE TIPS OF
THE FINGERS OVERLAP; THE HANDS ARE CLOSE
BUT THERE IS NO TOUCHING.

THE RIGHT FOOT IS FLAT, AND YOU ARE UP ON
THE BALL OF THE LEFT FOOT. WEIGHT IS EVENLY
DISTRIBUTED BETWEEN THE TWO FEET.

NOTE THAT ARMS ARE PARALLEL TO THE
GROUND, MEANING THE ELBOWS ARE HELD AS
HIGH AS THE HANDS.

COMMENT: There should be no thinking while this
meditative pose is held. About 3 minutes is enough
after the Rocking Motion. If the pose is taken after
all practice is finished, it should be held at least 5
minutes, or more.

Fig. 1

Fig. 2

120

INDIAN DANCE

NOTE: It is great fun to do T'AI CHI CHIH to music. Sometimes, when music of India is played, we can place the feet one in front of the other (Figures 1 and 2), pointing directly sideways, and do "Pulling Taffy" from these two positions, stepping forward from position of Figure 1 to that of Figure 2 — and vice versa — after each pull of the hands sideways.

If the practiser will experiement with different kinds of music, particularly of a folk nature, he will find it is an exhilarating experience, alone or in a group, to do these movements to music.

PART THREE

EPILOGUE

LET'S TALK ABOUT ENERGY FOR A BIT. WHILE FOOD IS NECESSARY, AND WE DO DERIVE SOME VITALITY FROM IT, THE TRUE ENERGY IS THE RESULT OF THE 'CHI' (PRANA). IF IT WAS ONLY A MATTER OF FOOD, A FAT PERSON, OR ONE WHO ATE GREAT QUANTITIES, WOULD BE THE MOST ENERGETIC. BUT, IS THIS THE CASE? OVERWEIGHT PEOPLE ARE APT TO BE LETHARGIC. WHO WINS THE MARATON RACE IN THE OLYMPIC GAMES, A FAT PERSON? HARDLY. IT ALWAYS SEEMS TO BE A SPARE, UNDERWEIGHT MAN DESCRIBED AS "WIRY".

IT WOULD BE INTERESTING TO PUT SOME ATHLETES ON A PROGRAM STIMULATING MAXIMUM 'CHI'. THE PRIMARY PRACTICE WOULD BE 'T'AI CHI CHIH', AND WE WOULD ADD THE SECRET 'NEI KUNG' (PRACTISED WHILE LYING ON THE BACK), AS WELL AS CERTAIN BREATHING AND MEDITATIVE TECHNIQUES. IT IS MY GUESS THAT A TRACKMAN WOULD THEN FIND HE COULD SURPASS HIS BEST PREVIOUS TIME FOR THE DISTANCE HE RUNS, AND HE WOULD REACH A NEW PLATEAU OF PERFORMANCE. IN SUCH SPORTS AS BASKETBALL, AN OLDER PLAYER MIGHT FIND HE TIRED LESS READILY AND WAS NOT AS SUSCEPTIBLE TO THE LEG INJURIES THAT PLAGUE BASKETBALL PLAYERS. A TENNIS PLAYER WOULD, I BELIEVE, NOTICE THE DIFFERENCE IN STAMINA IN THE FOURTH AND FIFTH SETS OF LONG MATCHES, AND WEIGHT-LIFTERS OR SHOT-PUTTERS WOULD FIND THEY COULD IMPROVE THEIR BEST PREVIOUS MARKS. I HAVE NEVER

MADE THESE EXPERIMENTS, BUT AM CONFIDENT THAT AN
INCREASE IN THE 'CHI', AND BETTER CIRCULATION OF IT,
WOULD READILY ACCOMPLISH THESE IMPROVEMENTS. I
HAVE NO DOUBTS AT ALL OF THE RESULTING IMPROVEMENT
IN PHYSICAL FITNESS.

MANY MEN FIND THEIR SEXUAL PERFORMANCE DIMIN-
ISHING FROM THE TIME OF THEIR MID-FORTIES. MUCH OF
THIS, OF COURSE, IS OFTEN PSYCHOLOGICAL, BUT THERE IS
USUALLY A DEFINITE PHYSICAL SLOWDOWN IN TODAY'S
SEDENTARY MAN AFTER HE REACHES HIS FORTIES. HOWEVER,
T'AI CHI TEACHERS IN THEIR EIGHTIES HAVE BEEN KNOWN
TO MARRY YOUNG WOMEN AND HAVE OFFSPRING. THE
CHINESE RESPECT T'AI CHI FOR ITS GREAT AID TO LONGE-
VITY. JUST AS IMPORTANT IS THE NECESSITY OF KEEPING
VIGOR AS ONE GROWS OLDER. CHINESE DOCTORS FOR SEVERAL
THOUSAND YEARS HAVE KNOWN THAT, WHEN THE 'YIN' AND
'YANG' ELEMENTS ARE OUT OF BALANCE, THERE IS ILLNESS,
AND THEY HAVE DEVELOPED TECHNIQUES, SUCH AS ACU-
PUNCTURE (INCLUDING MASSAGE AND MOXERY) TO RIGHT
THE IMBALANCE.

SO, WHEN WE LACK ENERGY, ARE CHRONICALLY TIRED
AND LACKADAISICAL, THERE IS A GOOD CHANCE THE
INTRINSIC ENERGY IS NOT CIRCULATING.

IN AN EXCELLENT PAMPHLET, REPRINTED FROM CHINESE
CULTURE OF MARCH, 1969, THE EMINENT TEACHER, PROF.
WEN-SHAN HUANG, SAYS:

"WE SEEM TO REALIZE THAT, IN THE UNIVERSE, THERE
IS AN EVER-ACTIVE EVER-CREATIVE LIFE, AND AN INEXHAUS-
TIBLE SOURCE OF ENERGY-LIFE AND ENERGY, WHICH ARE
MADE AVAILABLE TO MANKIND WHEN A FITTING STAGE OF
DEVELOPMENT IS ACHIEVED. IT IS PARTICULARLY SIGNIFICANT
THAT IT HAS A GREAT REVERENCE FOR LIFE." SO WE DISCERN
A SPIRITUAL BASIS FOR THIS GREAT 'CHI' ENERGY, WHICH IS
NOT OURS ALONE BUT BELONGS TO THE COSMOS (WE MANIFEST
IT INDIVIDUALLY WHEN WE DO THE NECESSARY DISCIPLINES TO

DEVELOP AND FOCUS THIS GREAT POWER).

PROF. HUANG CONTINUES: "T'AI CHI (SUPREME ULTIMATE) IS ORIGINALLY CIRCULAR IN SHAPE, AND IT IS THE COMBINED ENTITY OF THE YIN AND YANG PRINCIPLES."

THIS CIRCULARITY IS THE REASON WHY, IN ALL T'AI CHI DISCIPLINES, WE MOVE IN A CIRCULAR MANNER IN ORDER TO ACTIVATE THIS ENERGY. A WINDMILL FOLLOWS THE SAME PRINCIPLE.

"THERE IS, BEHIND THE PHENOMENON OF CHANGE, THE CHANGELESS ABSOLUTE, OR GRAND ULTIMATE (T'AI CHI)". FROM THIS WE COME TO REALIZE THAT, IN WORKING WITH THIS GREAT FORCE, WE ARE DOING MORE THAN MERE EXER- CISE — WE ARE PURSUING A WAY TO TRUTH, OR ENLIGHTEN- MENT. FEW REALIZE THAT ENLIGHTENMENT IS EXPERIENCED IN THE BODY, THOUGH THIS IS WHAT THE BUDDHA AND HIS SUCCESSORS HAVE ALWAYS TAUGHT AND EXPERIENCE SEEMS TO PROVE.

"T'AI CHI IS GENERATED FROM 'WU CHI', OR ULTIMATE NOTHINGNESS. IT IS THE MOVING POWER OF THE DYNAMIC AND STATIC STATES, AND THE SOURCE OF THE 'YIN' AND 'YANG' PRINCIPLES. WHEN THEY ARE IN MOTION, THEY SEPARATE, AND WHEN THEY REMAIN STATIC, THEY COMBINE. WE CAN UNDERSTAND THAT . . . ALL ITS MOVEMENTS ARE IN THE PATTERNS OF THE CIRCULAR T'AI CHI DIAGRAM

AND THEY ARE EXPRESSED WITH CURVES EMPHASIZING THE PRINCIPLES OF YANG AND YIN, SUBSTANTIAL AND INSUBSTAN- TIAL MOTIONS, OPENING AND CLOSING MOOD, AND DYNAMIC AND STATIC STATE."

IN THE ABOVE STATEMENTS, PROF. HUANG HAS QUOTED CHINESE AUTHORITIES OF ANTIQUITY, AND THE PRINCIPLES APPLY EQUALLY WELL TO T'AI CHI CH'UAN OR 'T'AI CHI CHIH'.

PROF. HUANG REFERS TO 'WU CHI' (SUNYATA IN SANSKRIT), OR ULTIMATE NOTHINGNESS. WHETHER WE CALL THIS NOTHING- NESS, VOID, GOD, OR BUDDHA NATURE, WE ARE DEALING WITH

126

THE SAME GREAT REALITY. JUST AS YOGA ATTEMPTS TO RETRACE ITS STEPS SO AS TO GET BACK TO THE SEED, OR CAUSE, IN T'AI CHI PRACTICE WE RE-INTEGRATE BY USING OUR MOVEMENTS TO TAKE US BACK TO THE SOURCE. IT IS GOOD IF, AFTER A PERIOD OF MOVEMENT, WE DO A SHORT MEDITATION, SUCH AS THE COSMIC CONSCIOUSNESS POSE OR SUCH AS THE ONE DELINEATED IN A FOLLOWING CHAPTER, IN ORDER TO BE QUIET AND CENTERED WHILE THE GREAT YIN AND YANG FORCES, WHICH WE HAVE SEPARATED AND CIRCULATED WITH OUR MOVEMENTS, COME TOGETHER AGAIN. A VERY YOUNG AND GREAT CHINESE METAPHYSICIAN, WANG PI (3rd CENTURY A. D.) HAS POSTULATED:

"MOTION CANNOT CONTROL MOTION. THAT WHICH CONTROLS THE MOTION OF THE WORLD IS ABSOLUTELY ONE!"

THE QUIET MEDITATION WE ENJOY IMMEDIATELY AFTER 'T'AI CHI CHIH' PRACTICE, WHILE OUR FINGERS, HANDS, AND BEING ARE STILL VIBRATING, IS A WAY TO RETRACE OUR STEPS TO THIS ONE THAT IS THE SOURCE. WE DO NOT HAVE TO BE RELIGIOUS TO DO THIS. IN THIS WAY WE CAN MAKE OURSELVES WHOLE TO GO ALONG WITH THE GREAT PHYSICAL BENEFITS WE CAN DERIVE FROM 'T'AI CHI CHIH' PRACTICE.

IT IS ENTIRELY POSSIBLE TO DO THE HAND MOVEMENTS OF 'T'AI CHI CHIH' WHILE WE ARE WATCHING TELEVISION OR SITTING IN AN UPRIGHT CHAIR — WE SIMPLY PLACE THE APPROPRIATE LEG IN A SLIGHTLY OUTSTRETCHED POSITION TO SIMULATE THE CORRECT STANCE. A DEFINITE FLOW OF 'CHI' ENERGY CAN BE STIMULATED IN THIS MANNER.

WHILE WALKING DOWN THE STREET, I OFTEN FIND THAT, UNCONSCIOUSLY, I AM PERFORMING THE 'T'AI CHI CHIH' MOVEMENTS WITH MY HANDS — AND WITH GOOD RESULTS! MOST FREQUENTLY I SEEM TO DO THE "AROUND THE PLATTER" VARIATION, OR THE DIFFICULT "CIRCLES WITHIN

CIRCLES" MOVEMENT.

DO NOT BE STARTLED BY THE FLOW OF ENERGY, EVEN IF IT IS FELT AS A HEAT CURRENT AT NIGHT AND WAKES YOU UP. GO WITH THIS FLOW — REST IN IT AND ENJOY IT. SAGES HAVE SAID IT IS THE "REAL", AND THEY BELIEVED DEVELOPMENT OF IT LED TO LONG LIFE. AFTER CONTINUED PRACTICE, THE READER SHOULD BE ABLE TO ESTIMATE SUCH BENEFITS FOR HIMSELF.

GREAT CIRCLE MEDITATION

IF THE READER WOULD LIKE TO SUPPLEMENT HIS 'T'AI CHI CHIH' WITH A SUITABLE MEDITATION, TO BRING ABOUT AN INNER STILLNESS AFTER THE MOVEMENTS HE HAS BEEN PRACTISING, THIS ONE IS AN EASY ONE TO PRACTISE AND SHOULD HAVE GREAT BENEFITS. CARRIED TO THE EXTREME, IT COULD BE A WAY TO ENLIGHTENMENT. SOMEWHAT SIMILAR METHODS WERE, EUPHEMISTICALLY SPEAKING, THE "WAY TO IMMORTALITY" PRACTISED BY ANCIENT TAOISTS.

INSTRUCTION:

SEAT YOURSELF IN AN UPRIGHT CHAIR, WITH THE BACKBONE HELD STRAIGHT (THOSE USED TO SITTING IN ANY CROSS-LEGGED POSITION, SUCH AS THE FULL OR HALF-LOTUS, SHOULD, OF COURSE, TAKE THAT POSITION). AFTER A MOMENT OR TWO OF SILENCE, WITH THE EYES CLOSED, ADJUST THE BREATH SO THAT IT IS FLOWING EVENLY, PUSH THE TONGUE AGAINST THE PALATE (ROOF OF THE MOUTH), AND OPEN THE NOSTRILS WIDE.

NOW WE ARE GOING TO TAKE A CURRENT UP THE SPINE AND DOWN THE FRONT. TO MAKE IT EASIER TO FEEL, LET'S VISUALIZE IT AS A WARM, GOLDEN, SLIGHTLY MOIST LIGHT.

FIRST, CONCENTRATE ON THE BASE OF THE SPINE (THE TAILBONE). THEN, LIFT THIS WARM, GOLDEN LIGHT SLOWLY UP THE BACKBONE. FIRST, THE SMALL OF THE BACK, THEN THE CENTRAL PART, THE SHOULDER BLADES, THE SHOULDERS, THE NECK, AND THE BASE OF THE SKULL — THRILLING EACH CELL, AS THE CURRENT PASSES THRU, WITH THE WARM, GOLDEN FEELING.

NEXT, THE LIGHT REACHES THE TOP OF THE HEAD, AND WE LET IT REST THERE FOR A FEW MOMENTS, THE WARM, GOLDEN FEELING SPLASHING DOWN OVER THE TOP OF THE SKULL AND BATHING US IN ITS SLIGHTLY MOIST, HEALING EFFULGENCE.

AFTER HOLDING THE LIGHT AT THE TOP OF THE HEAD FOR A SHORT WHILE, BRING IT SLOWLY DOWN THE FRONT — PAST THE EYES, THE NOSE, THE MOUTH, THE CHIN, AND ON TO THE NECK; THEN, TO THE CHEST, THE HEART REGION, AND THE ABDOMEN. FINALLY, IT REACHES THE SPOT TWO INCHES BELOW THE NAVEL (THE T'AN T'IEN, OR SEAT OF HEAVEN), WHERE WE LET IT STAY FOR A FEW MINUTES, FEELING THE WARM, GOLDEN CURRENT THERE, BUT MAKING NO EFFORT TO THINK ABOUT ANYTHING.

NOW WE ARE GOING TO ADD TWO DEVICES TO MAKE IT EASIER TO BRING THIS WARM, GOLDEN CURRENT UP THE SPINE.

(1)   AS WE MOVE IT UP FROM THE TAILBONE, WE SLOWLY INHALE. BY THE TIME THE CURRENT REACHES THE TOP OF THE HEAD, OUR CHEST IS EXPANDED AND HOLDING ITS FULL CAPACITY OF AIR.

HOLD THE BREATH FOR A COMFORTABLE WHILE. LET THE LIGHT SPLATTER DOWN OVER THE TOP OF THE HEAD AS WE HOLD THE BREATH, BEFORE STARTING DOWN.

(2)   AS WE INHALE AND MOVE THE LIGHT UP THE SPINE, GRADUALLY RAISE THE EYES FROM THE SPOT BELOW THE NAVEL, UNTIL THEY ARE POINTED UP TOWARD THE TOP OF THE HEAD AT THE TIME THE CURRENT REACHES THERE AND THE BREATH IS FULL. IN OTHER WORDS, WE USE THE EYES AS A ROPE, OR LEVER, TO GRADUALLY LIFT THE BREATH AND THE CURRENT, THE THREE ACTING TOGETHER. THIS SHOULD MAKE IT MUCH EASIER TO GET THE CURRENT TO THE TOP OF THE HEAD (THE "THOUSAND-PETALED LOTUS").

AFTER HOLDING THE BREATH FOR A LITTLE WHILE,
AS THE EYES ARE POINTED UP AND THE CURRENT IS AT
THE TOP OF THE SKULL, WE GRADUALLY BEGIN TO LOWER
IT DOWN THE FRONT, AT THE SAME TIME SLOWLY DROPPING
OUR EYES (WHICH ARE STILL CLOSED). AS THE BREATH IS
GRADUALLY LET OUT, WE ARE CAREFUL NOT TO DO IT IN
ONE LONG GASP, AS THIS WOULD CALL FOR AN IMMEDIATE
REFLEX IN-BREATH. RATHER, WE LET IT OUT IN "SECTIONS",
AND, WHEN THE LIGHT IS BACK DOWN AT THE T'AN T'IEN,
THE EYES ARE POINTING AT THE SPOT BELOW THE NAVEL
AND THE BREATH HAS COME TO REST. IF IT FEELS AS IF
WE ARE ABOUT TO BREATHE IN AT ONCE, SIMPLY FORCE
MORE AIR OUT AND COME TO REST. THIS PERIOD OF
RESTING THE CURRENT IN THE T'AN T'IEN, WITH THE AIR
OUT, IS AN IMPORTANT ONE. WE ARE BETWEEN BREATHS
AND, APPARENTLY, BETWEEN THOUGHTS. MAKE IT A PERIOD
OF NO MENTAL ACTIVITY AS WE REST IN "OURSELVES".
THIS IS THE FULL MEDITATION, AND IT IS SUGGESTED WE
MAKE THE FULL CIRCLE NINE TIMES, EACH TIME RESTING
AT THE T'AN T'IEN BELOW THE NAVEL.

WE CAN MAKE A LARGER CIRCLE BY STARTING THE
BREATH AT OUR FEET. IN THIS CASE, WE "BREATHE" IN
THRU THE SOLES OF THE FEET (THE "HSUEH", OR
"BUBBLING SPRING") AND TAKE THE CURRENT UP THE
INSIDE OF THE TWO LEGS, BEFORE WE BRING IT TOGETHER
AT THE T'AN T'IEN, AND THEN THRU THE OPENING BETWEEN
THE LEGS AND BEGIN THE TRIP UP THE SPINE.

IN SOME ESOTERIC PRACTICE, WE "BREATHE" IN THRU
THE SEXUAL ORGAN BEFORE GOING THRU THE SPACE
BETWEEN THE LEGS AND UP THE BACK.

IF DESIRED, WHEN WE ARE HOLDING THE LIGHT AT THE
TOP OF THE HEAD, WITH THE BREATH HELD IN, WE CAN,
MENTALLY (EYES STILL CLOSED AND POINTING UP) REPEAT
A MANTRA OR AFFIRMATION. "JOY, JOY, JOYOUS JOY"
WOULD BE A GOOD AFFIRMATION, OR JUST THE WORD "JOY".
WE CAN INSERT ANY POSITIVE STATEMENT WE WANT AT

THIS POINT. IT IS AN EFFECTIVE TIME TO DO SO.

PRACTISED REGULARLY, THIS MEDITATION CAN BRING GREAT BENEFIT. IT IS UP TO THE READER WHETHER HE WANTS TO TAKE THE TIME TO PRACTISE IT ONCE OR TWICE A DAY AFTER DOING 'T'AI CHI CHIH'. INCIDENTALLY, AT A BORING LECTURE OR GATHERING, OR ANY TIME ONE CAN BE SILENT FOR A FEW MINUTES (AS ON A TRAIN OR PLANE), IT IS EASY TO CLOSE THE EYES AND DO THIS BENEFICIAL MEDITATION.